Race Relations in the Primary School

Cecile Wright

David Fulton Publishers
London

David Fulton Publishers Ltd
2 Barbon Close, London WC1N 3JX

First published in Great Britain by
David Fulton Publishers 1992

Note: The right of the author to be identified as the author of this work has been asserted by her in accordance with the Copyright, Designs and Patents Act 1988.

British Library Cataloguing in Publication Data

A catalogue record for this book is
available from the British Library

ISBN 1-85346-142-3

Typeset by Chapterhouse, Formby L37 3PX
Printed in Great Britain by BPCC Wheatons, Exeter

Contents

Acknowledgements

The research on which this book is based was carried out on behalf of, and funded by, the Commission for Racial Equality, during 1987–9.

The project could not have been undertaken without the cooperation of the LEA, the staff of the schools, the children and parents, who cannot be identified by name since a condition of the research was that their confidentiality should be preserved. My most grateful thanks are nonetheless due to all of them. I would like to express my gratitude to both Rachel Whatley and Marjorie Richardson for their hard work in typing the manuscript.

Above all I'd like to thank Clive and Timothy for their unstinting support. To this end I dedicate this book to both of them, with my love.

Foreword

This is an important and timely book. Many of the ideas and themes which emerge have developed over a number of years as a result of Dr. Wright's direct involvement as a participant observer in both secondary and primary classrooms. Her earlier research, carried out on behalf of the Swann Committee, has been well publicised; but her account of the study of Race Relations in Primary Classrooms appears here for the first time.

The reader will find some of the descriptions of classroom events disturbing and thought-provoking. In my view it would be a pity if the book was to be viewed by teachers as another example of researchers seeking to identify classroom practices which show the teaching profession in a poor light. In many of the situations described in the book, the teachers appear to be as much the victims as are the pupils and their parents.

Dr. Wright did not set out to study examples of poor multi-cultural practice. Indeed schools were chosen by the local authority concerned because they were felt to reflect some of the more positive achievements in this field. What perhaps may be the most significant feature of Dr. Wright's study is that the pupils studied belonged to a first generation of parents who had themselves probably passed through similar primary schools just over a decade earlier, schools which also had espoused a multi-cultural curriculum. These parents appeared to have found their own experience of similar schooling inadequate. It was their scepticism of the value of such schooling that prompted such strong reaction and which teachers found difficult at times to cope with or understand.

If this view is the correct one, then, as more and more young black parents bring their own children to the schools which earlier had failed them, the kinds of problems and difficulties described by Dr. Wright will increase. If solutions to such problems are to be found, then the academic debate between those who support multi-cultural and those who support anti-racist approaches to schooling will need to be put on one side and more radical solutions examined. Such solutions must begin by those responsible for running our schools listening more carefully to what parents have to say rather than seeking to impose their own preconceived programmes of reform. Anyone reading Dr. Wright's book will surely realise the urgency of this task.

Professor Maurice Galton
University of Leicester
May 1992

List of Figures

CHAPTER ONE

Introduction

'It is difficult to get a reliable picture of the state of race relations in schools' claimed Her Majesty's Inspectorate in 1984. Subsequent work, notably the report of the Swann Committee, talked of poor 'race relations' both in multiracial schools and schools with few black children. Indeed, this phenomenon was considered to be one of the obstacles to black children's educational success. Yet the Swann Committee has provided very little discernible evidence to demonstrate the form that poor 'race relations' takes within schools. In recent years there have been a few studies, mainly in secondary schools, which have explored teacher and pupil attitudes and relationships within the multiracial context (Wright, 1986; Mac an Ghaill, 1988; Gillborn 1990). Peter Green's (1985) study of the social relationship between black children and their teachers is the only detailed empirical work on inter-ethnic relations with primary schools (this study will be looked at in greater detail in the next chapter). The paucity of research, therefore, on teacher–pupil interaction, teacher expectation and social relationships between pupils, particularly in the multiracial school context, confirms the HMI's claim that 'little is actually known about race relations in schools' (HMI, 1984, p. 1).

This book therefore is essentially concerned with exploring the relationships between black children, their white peers and staff during the earlier years of schooling.

It is pertinent at this stage to comment on the use of the term 'race-relations' as a discourse. The label 'race relations' is distinctly controversial. There exists a proliferation of theories of 'race relations' yet there seems to be little agreement amongst scholars (see, for example,

1

the discussions by Rex and Mason, 1986). Further, as an analytical term 'race relations' is disapproved of by scholars because it is frequently overgeneralised in ways which serve to support traditional stereotypes. (For a good discussion of the term 'race relations' see, for example, Miles, 1982; 1987; 1988 and Gilroy, 1987).

A crucial aspect of the controversy surrounding the term 'race relations' concerns the dubious concept of 'race'. The term 'race' principally arose out of 'pseudo scientific' doctrines of the nineteenth century advanced in Britain and Europe, which attempted to develop elaborate racial classifications and even theories of history on the supposedly 'scientific' assumption that human beings were naturally divided into discrete 'races', each with distinctive physical features (such as skin colour, hair texture and so on). Furthermore, these distinctive physical properties were used as a basis for explaining or inferring human behaviour or actions. These doctrines generally assumed that the different 'race' so defined could be hierarchically ordered and in that hierarchy the 'white' races were inherently superior to the 'non white' races. These theories of 'race', supposedly scientific claims, have been thoroughly discredited by modern biological science (for a sound discussion of this see, for example, Banton and Harwood, 1975; Husband, 1982). However, the act of classifying people according to discrete racial groups, and also inferring people's behaviour on the basis of specific biological properties, remains a great motivating force behind people's thought and action. In the field of education, for instance, the assumed relationship between 'race' and mental ability continues to occupy a place in educational discourse. It is recognised, for example, that the view of a relation between 'race' and intelligence is still wide-spread amongst teachers. Principally, for this very reason, the Swann Report considered it necessary to examine the 'IQ (intelligence quotient) question' at length in an attempt to discount it.

In contemporary Britain the notion of 'race', therefore, is not a viable biological concept, which is why it is now common for the term to be used in quotation marks. 'Race' has become a metaphor, the meaning of which reflects socio-cultural characteristics such as language, religion, custom, mores and life-styles, thus emphasising social characteristics rather than genetic endowment. It is these aspects which underlie the current usage of the term 'race relations'.

There has been a trend over recent years to use the term 'race relations' synonymously with the term 'ethnic relations'. The latter term embraces cultural identity, language, religion characteristics.

The distinctive feature of an ethnic group, therefore, is not its physical appearance, but its shared cultural heritage and values. Essentially, the former term is used in the title of this book because of wide currency in contemporary Britain.

Although this book's central concern is in within-school processes, this is not to disregard the possible influences of factors operating outside the school. It is recognised that the complex nature of society is such that the structures of economic and political power interrelate with people's actions. Consequently, the relationship found in school cannot be fully understood without reference to apparent economic, gender and racial inequalities operating in society generally. Thus, there is a recognition of the complex 'dialectic between school and society', and, in particular, the means by which inequalities transmitted into the school are modified, re-created or reinforced through its workings.

Before considering the organisation of this book it may be useful to outline both the research and the context on which it is based; and the research methodology which informed the study.

The context of the study

The material in this book is drawn from an ethnographic study (between 1988 and 1990) of four inner-city primary schools in one local education authority (LEA), which in order to preserve its anonymity will be called Hillsfield City. The four schools, which are given the pseudonyms Adelle, Bridgeway, Castle and Dewry respectively, drew on catchment areas which shared similar features (e.g. socio economic characteristics). The census data (1981) revealed that the areas constituted predominantly unskilled manual workers and are characterised by high levels of unemployment. Further, information recorded by each of the schools regarding the children's social backgrounds confirmed the census findings.

According to census figures, the catchment area for Adelle School contains six per cent of the Hillsfield City's black population, originating from the following country of birth: West Indies (12%); Pakistan and Bangladesh (8%); India (4%); and United Kingdom (76%). This is an area of mixed council and private housing.

Bridgeway School, Castle School and Dewry School shared the same catchment area. This catchment area contains 16 per cent of Hillsfield City's black populations, originating from the following country of birth: West Indies (22%); Pakistan and Bangladesh (18%);

India (10%); and United Kingdom (50%). The housing in this area is mostly large post-war council housing estate, with over 80 per cent of children entitled to free school meals.

The LEA's multicultural policy

Hillsfield City had formulated a policy statement on multicultural education, in which it stated the following 'objectives' and 'Framework for Action':

Hillsfield City Council declared that it acknowledges and welcomes the fact that it serves a culturally diverse community. In seeking to promote a positive attitude to this diversity, it recognises the crucial role of education provision. It therefore wishes to make a clear statement of policy objectives on education for a multicultural society.

Objectives

The City Council considers that these goals can best be achieved within a framework in which the following objectives are initially given priority:

  (i) to promote understanding, throughout the education service, of the different cultures found in Britain today, and to prepare all individuals for life in a 'plural' society where diversity is welcomed;
 (ii) to define and combat discrimination and racism, whether overt, unintentional or institutional;
(iii) to meet the needs of all children with particular regard to their cultural background, religion and language. This may require positive discrimination.

It cannot be emphasised too strongly that these objectives should be the concern of all members of the education service, both inside and outside schools.

A Framework for Action

Progress has already been made in the education service in order to achieve the above objectives. If further progress is to be made it is felt that the following should be included in a Framework for Action:

  (i) Initiation of and support for curriculum development relevant to a multi-ethnic society in all schools. Particular consideration should be given to the processes by which change can most effectively be achieved in this context.
 (ii) Support of identifying and countering direct and indirect discrimination in the education system against members of minority ethnic groups, and for combating all forms of racism.
(iii) Increased provision to assess and meet the particular needs of children from the minority ethnic communities.
(iv) Provision, as a priority, of in-service teacher education and support for schools to consider the implications of a multi-ethnic society for all children, and the particular needs of children from the minority ethnic community.
 (v) Developing and improving the links schools have formed with minority ethnic communities.
(vi) Positive consideration of ways of encouraging the recruitment and development of teachers from minority ethnic groups.
(vii) Further encouragement for the involvement of minority ethnic groups in the processes that shape the education service.

This policy has been augmented by the establishment of a Multicultural Centre and the appointment of advisory and support staff. The staff included advisory teachers for multicultural education, co-ordinators for multicultural education (primary and secondary), home/school liaison teachers, bilingual peripatetic and language support teachers.

In 1988, Hillsfield City and the local Council for Racial Equality conducted a survey on racial harassment in the city. This initiative resulted in the formulation of 'Policy Statement Against Racial Harassment' by the City Council, which took the form of an overarching policy to tackle incidents of racial harassment in all its services: housing, education, social services and so on. In its policy statement circulated to all schools and colleges the Education Department asserted the following:

The Education Department is committed to:

(1) equality in and entitlement to education for all people living in Hillsfield City, without racial harassment;
(2) recruiting a teaching and non-teaching staff which is aware of the injustice of racial harassment and is committed to end it;
(3) a curriculum which fully endorses and resources the right to a lifelong education for the whole population of Hillsfield City without racial harassment;
(4) promoting school and college-based democratic initiatives, working parties and forums against racism;
(5) requiring headteachers, teachers, non-teaching staff, LEA officers and advisers to assume an active responsibility to:

   (i) identify and report to proper authorities incidents of racial harassment;
   (ii) intervene to prevent all forms of racial harassment;
   (iii) organise systems, procedures and senior personnel to identify and investigate where appropriate in cases of racial harassment inside and outside the classroom;
   (iv) inform themselves on the nature of such harassment and work with students and parents to end it;
   (v) advise victims of harassment on their rights, and support and counsel them on how to redress their grievances;
   (vi) liaise with other agencies to provide support and take preventative measures.

General school background

It might be as well to begin by pointing to the fact that all four schools professed a commitment to the LEA's policy on multicultural education. Below each of the four schools is briefly described. The profile of both children and staff for the four schools during the period of the study is shown in Figure 1.1.

Figure 1.1 Staff and children on the school roll at Adelle, Bridgeway, Castle and Dewry

	Afro-Caribbean	Asian	White	Other
Teaching staff				
Adelle School	0	0	9	0
Bridgeway School	0	0	12	0
Castle School	0	0	10	0
Dewry School	0	0	13	0
Support staff				
Adelle School	0	0	0	0
Bridgeway School	1	1	1	0
Castle School	1	0	1	0
Dewry School	0	0	1	0
Nursery: teaching staff				
Adelle School	0	0	1	0
Bridgeway School	0	0	2	0
Castle School	0	0	2	0
Dewry School	—	—	—	—
Nursery: support staff				
Adelle School	0	0	2	0
Bridgeway School	1	1	2	0
Castle School	2	1	2	0
Dewry School	—	—	—	—
School pupils				
Adelle School	15	5	153	0
Bridgeway School	79	65	131	2
Castle School	54	37	79	0
Dewry School	37	37	111	3
Nursery children				
Adelle School	4	1	15	0
Bridgeway School	20	21	3	2
Castle School	13	8	44	0
Dewry School	—	—	—	—

ADELLE is a 3–8 school. It is a predominantly white school. Many of the children are from working class backgrounds. The school's catchment area borders on a mining community. The school is an old Victorian building. The school has an all-white female staff. A display of a variety of musical instruments constituted the range of multicultural images in the school. Many of the books available to the children reflect a multicultural theme. During the period of the study the school was frequently in contact with the LEA specialist services for multicultural education.

BRIDGEWAY is a 3–8 multiracial school, which serves a working class catchment area. The area is also characterised by high levels of unemployment. The school building is quite old, although modified somewhat over the years. Part of the modification was in order to establish a nursery unit in the school. The school has an all-female staff, black and white; all the teaching staff are white. The staff include a peripatetic English-as-a-second-language (ESL) teacher. There are several black nursery assistants who are used as support staff in the classroom. During the period of the study, the work of the children and photographs of school plays, events, black children and adults in various roles were displayed on the walls in the corridors and in the main hall. Displayed in the reception area was a multilingual 'welcome' notice. Careful thought was evidently given to the resources. They reflected positively the ethnic composition of the school. The school playground had been brightened by a mural of the different groups of children in the school at play.

CASTLE is a 3–8 multiracial school, the catchment area is predominantly working class. It has a detached nursery unit. Like the previous two schools, the school building is an old Victorian building. The school is staffed by an all-female staff. The teaching staff are all white; there are several black nursery assistants, who assisted the teacher in the classroom. The school's multiracial context was positively reflected in displays around the school, books offered to the children and the teaching materials used.

DEWRY is an 8–13 voluntary-aided multiracial middle working class. The staff is all-white. There is an equal proportion of male and female staff, but the headteacher, the deputy head and the senior staff are male. The staff include a peripatetic teacher whose principal role is to develop and deliver multicultural education in the school. A multilingual 'welcome to our school' notice displayed in the main entrance represented the only official acknowledgement of the school's multiracial context. A multicultural theme was evident also in the teaching materials used.

8

Methodology

The techniques of ethnographic research were used to record and interpret the routines and experiences of schooling (for details of ethnographic research methods, see Hammersley and Atkinson, 1983; Burgess, 1984; Woods, 1979; 1985). The research methods of ethnography are designed to portray a way of life as it is lived by a group of people. They require the researcher to be well acquainted with the group and to participate in the subjects' way of life for a considerable period of time. Stress is placed upon not disturbing the particular social setting, upon unobtrusive and 'naturalistic' methods, upon structural and open-ended interviews and conversations. With regard to the school, the researcher would actually enter the institution. The practitioner might observe life in classrooms, staffrooms and around the school such as the playground; and/or talk to those involved on a day-to-day basis (from the headteacher to the school's caretaker). Ethnographers claim to represent as accurately as possible the realities of the perspectives and the interaction of people in the group being studied.

By its very nature ethnographic work is rich in detail. Data are systematically collected and recorded and, building on the understanding which gradually develops, ethnographers, throughout the life of a study, constantly shift and reappraise their data before embarking on further rounds of data collection. In this respect, practitioners claim to get to the core of institutions, group life and activities, penetrating fronts of understanding; they try to relate these to social factors in the situation being studied so that types of ground theory are generated (Glaser and Strauss, 1967). Different participants see the same situation in different ways; the interaction between them may have consequences of which neither is fully cognisant. The ethnographer must not only understand the participants' perspectives but will also try to illuminate something of the wider processes.

I spent over a term in each school. This enabled me to build up a detailed, true-to-life picture of the groups under study in their schools, and the factors that bear on them in their various interrelationships. The main techniques used included observations, interviews (structured and unstructured) and conversations. Pupils and staff were seen and conversed with in many contexts and on many occasions. Both were observed in the classroom. I observed and chatted with children in the playground and joined in discussions with teachers in their staffroom, and attended staff meetings and INSET sessions. I accompanied pupils and staff on school trips. Fieldnotes were taken, a research diary kept and tape-recordings, where agreed, were made of interviews and lessons. I conducted interviews, some structured and others less so, with pupils, staff and parents.

Although observations and interviews were my most used methods, I made use of teachers' written classroom logs and existing documentary evidence within the schools (such as records of academic performance, referrals to withdrawal units, the Educational Psychological Services, school transfer records and so on). Such materials allow the researcher to compare different accounts and sources of information. Insufficient in isolation, together each source can reveal a detailed and critical picture of the processes at work at the level of the school.

Individual interviews were conducted with black and white parents. The interviews included a random sample of six white parents, four Afro-Caribbean and four Asian parents of Adelle school, and eight parents from each of the three groups for Bridgeway, Castle and Dewry. The age of the Afro-Caribbean parents ranged from early twenties and mid thirties compared with early twenties to over 40 for the white and Asian parents. The interview covered a variety of areas including parents' socio-economic and educational background, views on their child's school experience, the extent and nature of contacts with the school, satisfaction with the school. An interpreter assisted the researcher on a number of the interviews with Asian parents.

Contents of the book

Each chapter of the book deals with a particular issue which develops the overall picture of life in multiracial schools. The day-to-day interaction between staff and children and children themselves in various settings is the focus of Chapters 2 and 3. Chapter 2 describes and examines teacher–pupil interaction, peer relationships, discipline and control within the classroom settings. Chapter 3 looks at interactions in other settings such as the playground, particularly between auxiliary staff and children, and children themselves. Chapter 4 is concerned with looking at home-school relations. It explores teachers' perceptions of black parents; and also black and white minority parents' experiences, views and expectations of the school. The children's academic performance is examined in Chapter 5. The chapter aims to identify whether differences exist between groups of children in their academic performance.

Finally, Chapter 6 considers the implications for change and development highlighted by the issues explored in the previous chapters. It is particularly concerned with identifying a range of teaching and organisational initiatives which would be compatible with promoting 'good race relations' in the primary context and in the education system generally.

Note

'Black' as used in this chapter and throughout the book, refers to those of South Asian or Afro-Caribbean parentage.

CHAPTER 2

Into the Classroom

The classroom is regarded as the most important place in the education system; what happens there eventually decides how well the purposes of the system are achieved. Thus, it is in the classroom that the crucial face-to-face educational interaction occurs. Fundamental to the classroom context is the quality of the social relationships. The significance of this point is reflected in a spate of government reports during the 1980s conveying what might be termed the 'official' view of 'good' teaching and what promotes it. A report by HM Inspectorate, *The New Teacher and School* (DES, 1982) set the scene. Reporting on lessons observed, it was noted that successful lessons reflected good relationships between teachers and pupils. Teacher characteristics which were found to promote 'good' social relationships in the classroom were:

> ... a quiet, calm, relaxed, good-humoured attitude combined with firmness and a sense of purpose; a demonstration in interest in and knowledge of the pupils individually and an appropriate level of expectation of them; and the mutual respect ... the teacher being sensitive to the needs of the pupils and respecting their contributions, whatever their limitations. Where these qualities were shown, pupils were confident enough to play a full part in the lessons, to offer their own ideas and ask questions, or seek help when unsure, while the teacher could blend praise and encouragement with an occasional reprimand, the latter without arousing resentment. (pp. 6–7)

Part of the daily realities that children face in the classroom are working and interacting with classmates. Yet little is known about the

11

influences of peer-relations in the classroom. In fact, there has been a tendency to take this aspect of classroom reality for granted. The few available studies (Slavin, 1983) suggest that the social relationship between peers can be important in the promotion of education in the classroom and the child's own feelings of self worth. Essentially, if the child does not 'get along' with classmates, education may not be effective.

This chapter explores social relationships between children within the classroom.

Teacher–pupil interaction

The process of teacher–pupil interaction within the classroom has been the subject of a considerable amount of research. In contrast to the HMI report cited above, much of this research has indicated that social differentiation is a common feature of classroom life. Essentially, different groups of pupils in the same classroom, taught by the same teacher, may experience the classroom differently. Teachers' differential treatment of particular types of pupils has been well documented in respect of social class and gender.

Regarding social class, in a classic study by Rosenthal and Jacobson (1968), based on children attending an elementary school in a working class neighbourhood, teachers were systematically misled about the academic potential of their pupils. Teachers were encouraged to believe that certain pupils were expected to show marked gains in achievement in the forthcoming school years. It was found that these pupils made considerable gains on a number of educational measures during the year, gains which were not matched by those pupils who had not been identified as likely to do well. A further finding from the study was that teacher perceptions of the pupils who were expected to do well were more socially positive than those of their counterparts who were not expected to do well. However, if children did well who were not expected to, there were negative consequences, their teachers perceived them socially in negative terms. Further, this study gave rise to the theory that a 'self-fulfilling prophecy' was at work in many classrooms and that the under-achievement of working-class children could be accounted for partly by low teacher expectations. In another study, Rist (1970) suggested that the kindergarten teacher whom he studied used a 'roughly constructed ideal-type' based on social-class criteria with which to classify children into an hierarchical grouping system within her classroom – a 'caste system' as he put it. Consequent variation in teacher behaviour resulted in differences in child performance. In another study Sharp and Green's (1975) analysis of teacher ideologies and social control in the progressive Mapledene Infant School concerned itself with the formation of child identities through the teacher-structured processes of the classroom, in particular as an implication of the teachers' 'busyness ideology'. They concluded that:

> Whilst the teachers displayed a moral concern that every child matters, in practice there is a subtle process of sponsorship . . . where opportunity is . . . offered to some and closed off to others.

Similar claims have been made with regard to gender. Despite the evidence that within the classroom, boys rather than girls were likely to receive a greater amount of verbal commands, censure and criticism from both male and female teachers, and that girls are considered 'brighter' than boys (particularly at the primary level), in general teachers (of both sexes) tend to favour boys rather than girls. For instance, Clarricoates (1981) suggests that:

> In general, teachers find the boys more creative and more interesting to teach . . . In schools, girls' creativity is negated in favour of the creativity of boys which is seen as the only real and imaginative force within our male dominated culture.

As stated previously, evidence of racial differentiation in education generally and the classroom in particular is less well documented. This unexplored area was first ventured into by Peter Green. By analysing interaction in three junior and three middle schools Green (1985) was able to show that teachers, both male and female, who had highly ethnocentric attitudes, differentiated sharply in their attitudes between black pupils and whites. Green used the Flanders interaction analysis schedule to record systematically the interaction of white teachers with mixed pupil groups of 'West Indian', 'Asian' and 'European' pupils. Flanders' schedule is a way of systematically coding teacher behaviour and classroom events at regular intervals (see Flanders, 1970). The Flanders schedule system has been criticised for inflexibility and its inability to take account of non-verbal communications. Thus Green's findings, therefore, related to only a part of classroom life. Nonetheless, the study revealed that in the classroom boys of 'European' origin were particularly favoured. They were given a lot more individual teaching time than their numbers would warrant, and plenty of opportunity to introduce ideas into the flow of discussions. By contrast, 'West Indian' boys received much less individual attention and considerably less praise and encouragement. Teachers tended to treat 'West Indian' boys in a more restrictive way than others, issuing orders rather than encouraging them to express their feelings and ideas in the class.

This pattern was not repeated for 'West Indian' girls, who received less individual attention from male teachers than their size in the sample would have predicted.

> The girl of West Indian origin, whilst she is relatively ignored by her male teacher, appears to receive a more positive style of teaching than her male counterpart, who must at times wonder if there is anything more to classroom activity for him than criticisms, questions and directives. (Green, 1983b)

Overall, Green's findings indicated that both 'West Indian' boys and girls received more criticism than their 'Asian' and 'European' peers of the same sex, regardless of the teacher's gender (Green, 1983a). Green's findings suggest, therefore, that Afro-Caribbean pupils (especially boys) experience relatively more authoritarian and negative relationships with their teachers than their Asian and white classmates. Further, the study provides some indication of the combined effects of 'race' and gender classroom interaction. For instance, whilst white boys appeared to be the most favoured group in the classroom, in contrast, Afro-Caribbean boys were the least favoured. The study, however, gives little insight into the processes behind the teacher-pupil relationships. Consequently, it could be concluded that Afro-Caribbean boys' behaviour warranted the treatment received at the hands of their teacher. Recent ethnographic studies of multi-ethnic secondary schools (e.g. Wright, 1986, 1987; Mac an Ghail, 1988) which have shed some light on the processes operating in this context, however, suggest a different conclusion. Rather, these studies suggest that teacher expectations of different groups of children may work directly through the qualities of interactions in the classroom, thus affecting the kind of educational experience that children have.

Classroom differentiation is imbued with teachers' categorisation or teachers' typifications of the children they teach (see, for example, Rist, 1970; Leiter, 1974; Hargreaves et al., 1975; Sharp and Green, 1975). It is recognised that the use of typifications is a normal part of interaction in many social situations (Burrell and Morgan, 1979). The classroom context is considered to be conducive to this phenomenon. The obvious fact being that the teacher has to face and cope with a relatively large number of children. Given the teacher's occupational reality, typing is a means of reducing the complexity or, as Schutz (1970) states, 'making the world of everyday life "cognitively manageable" '. Thus the teacher simplifies by classifying. Related to the typification that teachers develop of pupils is the ideal pupil model or what Becker (1952) terms the 'ideal-client'. The notion of the ideal pupil is a construction which is likely to be drawn primarily from the lifestyle and culture of the teacher concerned.

The ideal pupil for teachers is likely to be a child who acts in ways which are supportive of teachers' interest-at-hand (Pollard, 1980), who enables them to cope and so on. Work by Becker (1952) and, more recently, Sharp and Green (1975) has suggested that teachers differentiate between pupils according to how closely they meet the ideal pupil criteria. All this occurs as part of the hidden curriculum. Children, therefore, tend to be classified and typed by the ways in which they vary from the ideal. For instance, social class factors have been found to be reflected in teachers' 'specifications' of the ideal pupil.

So far I have reviewed studies which have looked at the patterns of teacher–child interactions in the classroom. Studies suggest that stratification occurs within many classrooms, with teachers meting out different treatment to more or less favoured groups of pupils. I now wish to examine the pattern of teacher–child interaction observed in the four schools. My first impression of the schools in the study was that a pleasant atmosphere and a constructive relationship existed between staff and children. There was an emphasis on providing caring support and a friendly and encouraging environment for all the children. This approach was also reflected in the schools' pedagogic practice. There was a degree of sensitivity to the needs of the different groups of children as shown by the use of multicultural materials and images both inside and outside the classroom. The vast majority of the staff seemed genuinely committed to ideals of educational opportunity.

However, close classroom observation revealed subtle differences in the way white teachers treated black children. Differences in teachers' treatment of these children were observed both within the nursery and junior classrooms. I now examine the pattern of classroom interaction observed, firstly in relation to Asian children followed by a similar look at Afro-Caribbean children.

The Asian child in the classroom

In the nursery units the children came together as a group daily for 'story time' and (English) language work. Through effective discussion and questioning, the teacher encourages the children to extend their spoken English through talking about stories, objects, artefacts and singing.

In these formal sessions, the Asian children were generally observed to be excluded from the discussions because of the assumption that they could not understand or speak English. On the occasions when the Asian children were encouraged to participate in a group discussion, teachers often communicated with them using basic telegraphic language. When this strategy failed to get any responses the teachers would quickly lose patience with the children and would then ignore them.

This was also the observation of the black carers working in the nursery units, as the comment from Bridgeway First School reveals:

> They [white teacher and carers] have got this way of talking to them [Asian children] in a really simple way . . . cutting half the sentences – 'Me no do that' sort of thing . . . and that is not standard English. And they've [teachers] got this way of saying words, 'That naughty', and they miss words out and it really does seem stupid . . . I feel that it's not my place to say 'Well that's a silly way to speak to children . . .' I worry about what it tells the white children who think that the Asian children are odd anyway.'

Teachers often expressed open irritation or frustration when they believed that the Asian children's poor English language skills interfered with their teaching. The scenario below illustrates experiences common to the schools observed.

In a classroom in Adelle First School, five to six-year olds are working on a number of activities. The class teacher calls children out individually to listen to them read. She asks an Asian girl, recently arrived from Pakistan and in the school for less than a term, to come to her desk.

TEACHER: (*to Asian girl*) Right, let's see what you can do. (Teacher opens a book, pointing to a picture) This is a flower, say 'flower'.

REHANA (*nods nervously, appears a little confused*)

TEACHER: This is a flower. After me, flower.

REHANA (*no response*)

TEACHER: (*calls for assistance from one of the Asian pupils*) Zareeda, would you come here a minute. (*Zareeda walks over to the teacher's desk*) What is the Urdu word for 'flower'? (*Zareeda fidgets nervously*) Tell her in Urdu that this is a flower.

ZAREEDA: (*looks very embarrassed, refuses to speak. A few children gather around the teacher's desk. Zareeda hides her face from them*)

TEACHER: Zareeda, if you're embarrassed, whisper the word to me.
ZAREEDA (*no response*)
TEACHER: (*visibly irritated*) Well, Zareeda, you're supposed to be helping, that's not the attitude in this school, we help our friends. You're supposed to be helping me to teach Rehana English. (*to the Asian girls*) Go and sit down, both of you ... I'll go next door and see if one of those other Asian children can help me. (*Teacher leaves the room*)

The incident had attracted the attention of the whole class. Whilst the teacher was interacting with the Asian girls, the white children were overheard remarking disparagingly about 'Pakis'.

In the classroom many of the Asian children displayed a quiet and controlled demeanour; in comparison to other children they appeared subdued. There was a sense in which the Asian girls seemed invisible to the teachers. They received the least attention from the teacher in the classroom. They were rarely invited to answer questions and take a lead in activities in the classroom or other formal settings. Interestingly, for children of this age group, greater classroom co-operation was observed between Asian boys and girls than was the case for other pupil groups. In the classroom these children operated as an isolated group.

Such a reaction to their classroom experience was in itself perceived to be a problem by some teachers, as reflected in this comment from a teacher at Bridgeway First School:

The Asian children tend to be self-isolating. I have to deliberately separate that group. They tend to ignore all other children, are not too happy sitting next to anybody else, and see themselves as their own little group. They tend to converse in their own language. I'm afraid I have to say 'Now come on, stop.'

When asked to explain why Asian children conversing in their mother tongue in the classroom was a concern, she pointed out:

Because I don't know what is being said. It could be something against the other children in the class. I mean, I've no idea what is going on. Often one [Asian child] will come up to me to say 'Miss, he's swearing' kind of thing. They always tell on each other of course. But, no I don't encourage that, at least not in the normal classroom situation. They [Asian children] do go as a special group to Mrs R [English-as-a-second-language support teacher] and she does special stories in Urdu with them.

Among the negative responses to Asian children expressed by teachers was also open disapproval of aspects of their custom and tradition, which were considered to pose problems for classroom management. Such disapproval added to the negative experiences of school of some of these children precisely because of the apparent clash of school and home expectations.

Preparing for physical education lessons, for example, posed some difficulties for the Asian girls because pupils were required, particularly at the nursery school, to undress in the classroom. The girls employed a number of creative measures to acquire some privacy, such as hiding behind chairs or under desks. The teachers often showed total disregard for the feelings of these children, openly disapproving of what they considered was over-sensitive modest behaviour on the part of the Asian girls. At the end of the PE lesson the Asian girls were the recipients of teachers' sarcasm – 'Well, don't you wish you were all as quick getting undressed?'

The anguish experienced by the Asian girls was expressed by seven and eight year olds at Adelle First School:

ANJALI:	We don't like PE. I get a headache when we do PE.
BALBIR:	I don't like it because we are not allowed to do it.
INTERVIEWER:	Why?
ANJALI:	Because it's like my mum and dad said, her mum and dad, if you do PE you get Gonah.[1]
BALBIR:	We go to mosque and if you do PE, and you just go to mosque like that you get smacked from that lady. That's why we don't like to do PE. We don't want trouble from God for doing PE.
ANJALI:	Because we don't allow other people to see our pants, we hide behind the table when we get changed for PE.
INTERVIEWER:	What does the teacher say when you hide behind the table?
ANJALI:	Sometimes she shouts.
INTERVIEWER:	Have you told the teacher about your feelings?
ANJALI AND BALBIR:	No, no.
INTERVIEWER:	Why?
BALBIR:	Because we're scared.
ANJALI:	Because we don't like to, she would shout.

The children are expressing a fundamental conflict between the perceived expectations of their background and the requirements of the school. However, they were reluctant to share their feelings with the class teacher, because of the fear of being shouted at. Thus, the teacher was perceived as being unsupportive.

Another example where negative attitudes by a teacher failed to support Asian girls occurred when a class at Dewry Middle School was discussing a forthcoming weekend visit. The teacher was distributing letters to the class to take home to parents to elicit their permission. The teacher commented to the Asian girls in the class. 'I suppose we'll have problems with you girls. Is it worth me giving you a letter, because your parents don't allow you to be away from home overnight?'

The cumulative effects of teachers' attitudes towards Asian

children was to create a sense of insecurity for these children in the classroom. Moreover, the attitudes of the teachers influenced the Asian children's social disposition vis-à-vis their classroom peers. They were extremely unpopular, especially among their white peers. Indeed, as will be shown later in the chapter, children of other groups, particularly white children, would use aspects of the exchanges between the teacher and the Asian child that referred to perceived personal deficiencies to tease and taunt their Asian classmates.

The Afro-Caribbean child in the classroom

As with the Asian child, the Afro-Caribbean child carries a range of expectations of his or her behaviour and educational potential, right from the nursery class. While the Asian child may experience a pattern made up of assumed poor language skills (particularly in the case of the younger Asian child) and negativity towards their cultural background alongside expectations of educational attainment, the Afro-Caribbean child's experience is often largely composed of expectations of bad and disruptive behaviour along with disapproval, being 'shown up', public reprimands and punishments. Essentially, it was observed that whenever Afro-Caribbean children were present they were always amongst the most criticised and reprimanded children in the group. Moreover, there was a greater willingness for some teachers to reprimand Afro-Caribbean children (especially boys) for similar behaviour ignored when adopted by other children.

The experience of Marcus, a four-year old Afro-Caribbean boy attending the nursery at Castle First School exemplifies this observation. Marcus had been attending the nursery for a year, he was considered by the nursery staff to be 'a very able child', 'active', 'boisterous' and to exhibit behaviour which often bordered on being 'potentially disruptive'. Marcus was one of the few children in the nursery who seemed to mix freely with other groups of children. A classroom scenario of a whole group activity including the teacher and a group of five children (age four years) reported below, illustrates the frequent control and criticism experienced by Marcus in the classroom.

TEACHER: Let's do one song before home time.
PETER: [white boy] Humpty Dumpty.
TEACHER: No, I'm choosing today. Let's do something we have not done for a while. I know, we'll do the Autumn song. What about the Autumn song we sing. Don't shout out, put your hand up nicely.

MANDY:	(*shouting out*) Two little leaves on a tree.
TEACHER:	She's nearly right.
MARCUS:	[Afro-Caribbean boy with his hand up] I know.
TEACHER:	(*talking to the group*) Is she right when she says 'two little leaves on a tree'?
WHOLE GROUP:	No.
TEACHER:	What is it, Peter?
PETER:	Four.
TEACHER:	Nearly right.
MARCUS:	[Afro-Caribbean boy, waving his hand for attention] Five.
TEACHER:	Don't shout out Marcus, do you know Susan? [white girl]
SUSAN:	Five.
TEACHER:	(*holding up one hand*) Good, five, because we have got how many fingers on this hand?
WHOLE GROUP:	Five.
TEACHER:	Okay, let's only have one hand because we've only got five leaves. How many would we have if we had too many. Don't shout out, hands up.
MANDY:	(*shouting out*) One, two, three, four, five, six, seven, eight, nine, ten.
TEACHER:	Good. Okay, how many fingers have we got?
MARCUS:	Five.
TEACHER:	Don't shout out, Marcus, put your hand up. Deane, how many?
DEANE:	Five.
TEACHER:	That's right, we're going to use five today. What makes them dance about, these leaves?
PETER:	(*shouting out*) The wind.
TEACHER:	That's right. Ready here we go.

Teacher and children sing, Five little leaves so bright and gay, dancing about on a tree one day. The wind came blowing through the town, whoooo whoooo whoooo, one little leaf came tumbling down.

TEACHER:	How many have we got left?
DEANE:	(*shouting out*) One.
MARCUS:	(*raising his hand enthusiastically*) Four.
TEACHER:	(*to Marcus*) Shush. Let's count, one, two, three, four.
TEACHER:	How many, Deane?
DEANE:	Four.
TEACHER:	Good, right let's do the next bit.

Teacher and children sing the next two verses.

TEACHER:	How many have we got left, Peter?
PETER:	Don't know.
MANDY:	Two.
TEACHER:	I know that you know, Mandy.
MARCUS:	Two.
TEACHER:	(*stern voice*) I'm not asking you, I'm asking Peter, don't shout out. We'll help Peter, shall we. Look at my fingers – how many? One, two. How many Peter?
PETER:	Two.
TEACHER:	Very good. Let's do the next bit.

Teacher and children sing the next verse. At the end of the verse:

TEACHER: How many have we got left, Susan?
SUSAN: One.
TEACHER: Good, let's all count, one. Let's do the last bit.

Teacher and children sing the last verse; at the end of the verse:

TEACHER: How many have we got left?
ALL
CHILDREN: None.
TEACHER: That's right, there are no leaves left. Marcus, will you stop fidgeting and sit nicely.

In a conversation with the Afro-Caribbean child care assistant attached to the unit, about the above observation, she commented,

Marcus really likes answering questions about things. I can imagine he's quite good at that because he's always got plenty to say..., but they [white teachers] see the black children as a problem here.

Black and ethnic minority carers in the nursery unit at Bridgeway School also expressed concern about the attitudes of white colleagues towards Afro-Caribbean boys in particular. One child care assistant pointed out:

The head of the nursery is for ever saying how difficult it is to control the black children in the nursery, because they only responded to being hit . . . There is an attitude that they all get beaten up at home and they're all used to getting a good slap or a punch. There are one or two [black children] that they are quite positive about . . . they happen to be girls. I think it is a very sexist nursery. The black girls they are positive about are thought to be clean, well spoken, lovely personalities. As for the boys, I think boys like Joshua [Rastafarian] and Calvin, who have recently moved into the Reception Class, they were labelled disruptive. When Fay [Afro-Caribbean child care assistant] was there she really got these two children to settle, because they had somebody to relate to, that understood them, realised that they weren't troublemakers. They just needed somebody to settle them, especially Calvin, he related to her really well. Then just when he was settling down, they upped and took him [transferred to the Reception Class] . . . He went right back to stage one, he sat outside the classroom for the first few months of school apparently . . . all he used to do was sit outside the classroom. I used to go over to speak to him, I'd asked him what had happened. He used to say the teacher said, 'I've been naughty so she's put me outside.'

In contrast to the lack of attention which the Asian children often faced, Afro-Caribbean boys received a disproportionate amount of teachers' negative attentions. There was a tendency for Afro-Caribbean and white boys to engage in task avoidance behaviour in the classroom, to fool around when they should be working and to be generally disobedient. Teachers were observed to be more inclined to turn a blind eye to flagrant breaches of normal classroom standards when committed by white boys, or were observed to be lenient in their disapproval. By contrast, similar conduct on the part of Afro-Caribbean boys was rarely overlooked by the teachers. Disapproval was usually instant. The punitive sanctions employed by the teachers included verbal admonishment, exclusion from the class, sending children to the headteacher, or withdrawal of privileges. Afro-Caribbean boys were regularly the recipients of these punitive measures, which were often made a public matter. Such reprimands often went beyond discipline to become more of a personal attack on the individual child concerned as in the following example below from Bridgeway School involving Carl, an eight year-old Afro-Caribbean boy.

Carl was judged to be a very academically able child. Further information gathered both from his class teacher and the staffroom suggested that he was considered by the teachers to be arrogant, chauvinistic and disruptive in class but was also seen to be very popular among classmates and peers in general.

A class of seven to eight year-olds settled down to work after morning break. The children were seated four to a table. The classroom noise varied from low to medium. The teacher seated at her desk marking the children's work, kept a vigil on a table where the following four children sat: one Afro-Caribbean boy (Carl), two white boys and one white girl. Every time the classroom noise level increased, the teacher looked at the Afro-Caribbean boy, who worked effortlessly at the task set him, stopping occasionally to converse with the white boys seated at his table.

TEACHER: Carl, get on with your work.
CARL   (*Gave her a disparaging sideways glance. Attended to his work.*)
The classroom noise decreased temporarily. The classroom noise rose again. The teacher looked up from her marking and saw that Carl and the white boys seated at his table were engaged in task avoidance behaviour.
TEACHER: (*shouting*) Carl stop disrupting the class!
CARL: It's not only me (*pointing to his peers*), they're not working.
TEACHER: (*shouting*) Carl leave my class, go and work outside. I'm not having you disrupting the class.
Carl picked up his book and left the room, giving the teacher a disparaging sideways glance.
TEACHER: (*addressing the class*) Look at that face (*referring to Carl*). Go on outside. The trouble with you is that you have a chip on your shoulder.
Carl spent the remaining school day outside the classroom, working in the corridor.

In a conversation with the class teacher, she admitted that she had excluded Carl from the classroom on other occasions, against the policy of the school. The teacher appears not to be concerned that Carl's exclusion from the classroom meant that he could not participate in the lesson.

TEACHER: He stops me doing my job. I mean my job isn't a disciplinarian, or a perpetual nagger, my job is to teach and I'm not able to do that because of him constantly interrupting. If I'm not looking at him he'll do something terrible to make me.

INTERVIEWER: Have you shared your experience with the headteacher, for instance?

TEACHER: Yes, . . . I mean she has been very supportive but is unaware of the constant stress factor in the classroom, you know where you feel you need to eject that child from the classroom. But we're told not to put them outside, so the next thing is to send them to Mrs Y [headteacher]. I got to the point on Friday . . . that last half hour, I just thought there's no way – he'd get the better of me. So I sent him down to Mrs Y and I hadn't realised that Mrs Y wasn't in. So he sat there with the Secretary all the time, which I mean is a plus as far as that is concerned, my class gained the benefit of his absence. Carl's behaviour is a shocking problem. Now there are other children in the class with problems, a lot of it's behavioural, ever so much of it is learning difficulties and then you've got all that plus a bright one like Carl, you know its not a very good teaching/learning situation.

Another group of Afro-Caribbean children who seemed to be particularly prone to experiencing poor relations with their class teacher were those of Rastafarian background. During the study there were a very small proportion of Rastafarian children to be found mainly in Bridgeway School and Castle School respectively. At Bridgeway School there were two boys in both the nursery and school from this group, whilst at Castle School there were two boys and two girls in both the nursery and the school. Observations indicated that whenever Rastafarian children (especially the boys) were present in the class they were also always among the most criticised and controlled children in the group.

An Afro-Caribbean carer at Castle School expressed her considerable distress at the responses of white colleagues to a three year-old Rastafarian child who was having difficulty adjusting to the nursery environment. This child, on occasions, would lash out in frustration. She felt that her white colleagues were reluctant to accommodate his needs as they would normally do for a white child in a similar situation. As she states:

When Levi first came in [to the nursery] he did things. I got the feeling that Miss M [white teacher] resented him. Because he took up so much time. He had only just turned three. She used to say 'Well, I'm not going to waste my time like that'. And if Levi messed about I think sometimes the way she handled him made him do things. If a child is going to bite you or scratch you, you make sure they didn't. You'd hold their hand or you would stop them. She didn't, she just let him do it, then she'd flare up and walk across [to the school] and tell the head. In the end the head said we've got to keep a record of his behaviour, write down incidents. I just didn't write anything down. He's lashed out at me . . . he's come back to me the next day and said sorry about what he's done. And I think – fair enough. He's only a child. I just think Miss M blows it up. I don't see him as a problem. Confidential notes are kept on him. I don't think his mother knows. What upsets me about it is that when this first happened, the reason why the head said that she wanted to keep records on things that he'd done, was in case he ever needs statementing.[2] She would have the evidence. I was really upset, he's three. I'm really glad that Levi behaves the way he does, he says 'sorry' whenever he does things . . . Only bad things go in this book . . . I never write in this book. I don't agree with them [colleagues] because you don't know who's going to see it or where it's going to go.

As the Rastafarian children progressed through their primary career they were seen by some teachers as a particular threat to classroom management.

I would say that probably the black children, particularly the Rastafarian children, are taking the lead, in quite a lot, they are making the running quite often, but not in all cases. Those children I'm sure are being made particularly aware by their parents as regards racism. And there is a problem of a small child trying to negotiate a world which they have been made aware is a racist one. You know, they've got to watch out and actually finding out that their teacher is one. A teacher as one with so many children is quite vulnerable. I think it is very complex, because they're sort of getting their own back from a racist white world.

An example of this was given by the headteacher of Castle School recounting her experience with a four year-old Rastafarian boy. As with the teacher quoted above, she expresses a sensitivity to the child's experience of racism, but an apparent incomprehension in knowing how to tackle this.

He was in his first term in school so he was under five and he was vulgar in class. He had this habit of running wild and hurting other children and we actually removed him from the class before he actually hurt other children. So he had been removed and he came into my room where he didn't want to be and he was angry and he just screwed up his face and said, 'I hate you, I hate you, you are white . . . and you're not a Rasta'. He felt that I was getting at him because he was black, I think it was the first time I have actually confronted the issue and that's what I feel with several of the Rastafarian children in particular, that's what they see. So there is this enormous barrier because of who we are.

During the study, all the pupils observed in the classroom were individually interviewed, they were asked questions relating to their 'likes' and 'dislikes' about school. In their conversations many Afro-Caribbean and Rastafarian children identified their relationship with teachers as a special difficulty. More specifically, these pupils complained about unfair treatment, or being 'picked on'. A complaint which was often confirmed by their white classmates. Samuel, a seven year-old Afro-Caribbean child at Bridgeway School, talked of what he perceived to be the teachers' unfair treatment of other Afro-Caribbean pupils:

SAMUEL: I always get done and always get picked on... I want to go to a black school with all black teachers... it's better. I want to go to a school with just black people.

INTERVIEWER: Why?

SAMUEL: Because when you go to a school with white people they give you horrible food and you're always picked on when you don't do nothing. When it's white people they just say stop that and stop doing this.

INTERVIEWER: Are you saying that you would like some black teachers here (in the school)?

SAMUEL: Yes.

INTERVIEWER: Have you ever told anybody this, have you ever told the teachers?

SAMUEL: I haven't said that to any of the teachers... Because they'll be cross and say the white people just treat black people the same as other people. And one time someone hit Sheena [Afro-Caribbean child] and she was crying and if it was a white person and I said 'Miss she's crying' she would have went there straight away, but when it was Sheena, she [teacher] just ignored me. And she said 'Get in line' [asked by the teacher to join the queue] and I said [to the teacher] 'You only think about white people'. Then she [the teacher] told Mrs J [headteacher] and Mrs J started shouting her head off at me.

INTERVIEWER: So you felt that the teacher didn't do anything because Sheena was black?

SAMUEL: Yes, because if it was a white person, she would say 'What's the matter?' and then she would have said, 'What's up?' And when you hit 'em, if someone said it didn't hurt she [teacher] just say stand against the wall.

INTERVIEWER: Do you think the teacher treats black children differently to white children?

SAMUEL: Yes.

INTERVIEWER: In what ways?

SAMUEL: Because when it's black people, and they just run down the stairs. I mean when Martin [white boy], he ran off. She [teacher] said 'come back, stop at the door' and Martin didn't hear, Martin ran off. And then Richard told me that the teacher want us to come back to the classroom, so I walked back. Then I told on Martin, and Miss just told me to shut up, she said, 'Be quiet'.

INTERVIEWER: What about the Asian children, the Pakistani children, how do the teachers treat them?

SAMUEL: Treat them the same as black people.

INTERVIEWER: In what way?

SAMUEL: It's just that they [teachers] treat Pakistani people a little better than black people.

INTERVIEWER: Can you just tell my why you say that?

SAMUEL: Because every time anything goes wrong in class, and everyone's messing about around the carpet, they [teachers] call me out, Rick and Delroy [both Afro-Caribbean] and that. But they don't call out the white people and the Pakistani.

INTERVIEWER: How does this make you feel?

SAMUEL: *(long thoughtful pause)* Sad.

This view was also echoed by older children. An 11 year-old Afro-Caribbean child at Dewry School said:

BENJAMIN: My teacher can be all right, but other teachers irritate me a lot. This teacher called Miss L irritates me. When everybody's making a row in the hall, they call my name, instead of other people's . . . they don't like black people.

INTERVIEWER: What makes you say that your teachers don't like black people?

BENJAMIN: They don't because there's a girl in my class, Rita. There is only me and her in the class that's black Miss . . . She's always involving Mr P [the headteacher] a lot. Always going to see Mr P. It's always black children getting done. You know Rita's brother he was in trouble a lot, and it was always because of other kids, white kids . . . This white boy pushed Rita down the stairs. Now if it was me, I would have got detention. That boy never got detention. He went in the Head's room for about three minutes and came back out. The girl [Rita] was curled up on the floor in pain. You should have seen all her legs, cut up. And there's this prejudiced dinner lady that don't like blacks.

In addition to their perceived regular experience of reprimands, Afro-Caribbean children felt that the other teachers discriminated against them in the allocation of responsibility and rewards. A nine year-old Afro-Caribbean child at Dewry School said:

In the first school the teachers were really prejudiced. There was quite a lot of coloured people in the class and Miss B she'd never pick any coloured people to do a job and nearly all the white people got a biscuit, but the coloured people never. Like if a white person wanted to go to the toilet, she'd say yeah, but if a coloured person wanted to, she'd say no.

A teacher at Dewry School expressed her objection to being accused by the older Afro-Caribbean children of being prejudiced; she seemed impervious to the children's complaint . . .

I was accused of doing several things last year. 'I didn't like blacks'. 'You are only saying that because I'm black.' 'You wouldn't be picking on anyone else', this came particularly from Delroy, who has got a big chip on his shoulder. I think it's because his dad left and there is a lot of emotional instability there. But I objected to that . . . I am not saying that I am not me, I am sure that I respond to things in a very unfavourable way, but I am fighting it. I am not saying I am pristine and my halo is glowing, but at least I am aware of my own shortcomings and I do make positive steps to overcome what has been instilled in me for years. Whether or not things come out sort of unconsciously without me knowing. I am sure that if I knew things were coming out then I would take positive steps.

Many teachers seemed unaware of their disproportionate criticism and controlling statements directed at Afro-Caribbean pupils in the classroom. Indeed, most of the incidents witnessed in the classroom were not as clear-cut as the ones cited above. Yet the pattern of teacher-pupil interaction did not go unnoticed by the white children.

The Afro-Caribbean complaint about unfair treatment endured at the hands of their teachers was often confirmed by their white classmates:

SUSAN: [white, 11-years old] Teachers, they're prejudiced against blacks, especially Mr M.

INTERVIEWER: In what ways would you see prejudice happening?

SUSAN: Because sometimes if there's a black and white fighting in the playground, he'll [the teacher] bully the black and not the white. If white bully black, the black will get done for it.

INTERVIEWER: Why do you think that the black child will get done, as you say?

SUSAN: Because Mr M. and some of the other teachers are prejudiced. They don't like blacks against whites.... In assembly, if a black [child] and white [child] are talking, he'll [Mr M.] shout at the black, and tell him [pupil] to come out to the front.

In conversation with two white children (Ricky and Neil, both aged seven years, at Bridgeway School) both commented on the unfair treatment of their black peers and what they considered to be a link between black children's treatment and the school's staffing profile:

RICKY: There's all white teachers here.

NEIL: Except some people that come to help [the non teaching staff].

RICKY: All the teachers are white. Its only black people who help. Everyone else that's white is a teacher here ... There should be black teachers because there's more black people [pupils] and they won't get picked on so much.

INTERVIEWER: Are you saying that the black children are picked on?

NEIL: Yeah, they get done a lot in class for messing about ... and being 'cock of the school'.

INTERVIEWER: What's 'cock of the school'?

NEIL: Tough and all that.

It is evident, therefore, that an awareness of teachers' frequent criticism and control of Afro-Caribbean and Rastafarian pupils was not restricted to non-teaching staff, Afro-Caribbean and Rastafarian pupils themselves or to their white peers. As shown above, both the non-teaching staff and pupils reports were supported by classroom observation.

Discipline as control

However, the poor rapport observed between Afro-Caribbean children and their teachers represented only one aspect of Afro-

Caribbean and Rastafarian children's total experience of teachers. There were two further critical dimensions, the first concerned the use of physical restraint and the second concerned the application of the school's official disciplinary procedures. Each of these concerns are considered in turn.

Physical restraint as control

Observation of many lessons and conversations with teachers, showed there to be considerable concern among teachers, particularly at the multiracial schools, about perceived indiscipline in the classroom and having to constantly enforce order and control (a concern not borne out by observation). A concern which partly reflected teachers' belief, as shown above, that certain pupil groups posed a constant threat to classroom order (namely the Afro-Caribbean and Rastafarian children); and also teachers' expectations and perspectives on teaching in an inner-city school setting (both concerns will be explored further in this chapter under Teachers' perspectives).

Howard Becker (1952) in his study of teachers in Chicago has shed some light on the expectations, perspectives, coping strategies and practices employed by teachers teaching in 'slum' schools, catering for 'lower class' and black students. Further, it was found that teachers adopted practices which they would not have otherwise employed in 'good' schools in middle or upper class areas. This involved acquiring teaching and disciplinary techniques which enable them to deal adequately with 'slum' children. Becker also argued that teachers generally orientated their perspectives – that is, their view of how the job of teaching ought to be performed – around an image of the 'ideal client'. Children attending 'slum' schools were considered to present the greatest problems for teachers in terms of teaching itself, classroom discipline and 'moral acceptability'.

Classroom observation found similar processes, identified by Becker, to be operating in the study's schools. Regarding classroom discipline, several teachers were observed to resort to 'unofficial' measures in order to maintain classroom order. It was not uncommon, therefore, for teachers to apply physical restraint, where it was felt that directives and verbal admonishment failed to achieve the desired classroom control. The use of physical restraint used by the teachers ranged from prodding to smacking the child. Such measures were observed particularly in dealings with the Afro-Caribbean children of both sexes in the multiracial schools.

The headteacher at Bridgeway School's account of how she and a class teacher dealt with an Afro-Caribbean boy of six years, who had to be forcibly removed from the classroom for 'unacceptable behaviour', gives an indication of the sort of physical restraints/handling Afro-Caribbeans experienced at the hands of teachers and headteachers.

Vincent threw a tantrum and attacked Lisa [white girl]. He said that she called him some name and had hit him. As soon as he started, she [class teacher] decided to remove him from the classroom.

Fortunately, I had come upstairs, I could take over from her [the class teacher]. She had to drag him all that way [a distance of nine metres from the classroom]. (*Flippantly*) It's a good thing we have carpet on the floor or he would have been full of splinters and all. He refused to walk. Eventually I said 'get up and we'll go into the community room', 'No' he said. So I dragged him from there (*pointing to where the class teacher had left him*). He wouldn't get up so I just pulled him. When we got to this door [door of the community room] I just picked him up and I just flung him in that chair (*pointing to the armchair in the community room*). I held him, held his knees first of all, then I eventually picked him up and put him in my lap. I had his legs across me, and he was sort of doing this all the time [kicking his legs]. He struggled and struggled and struggled for a good quarter of an hour. I held his arm under the soft spot very tight, I wouldn't be surprised if he didn't have a bruise there because I had to hold him so tight to gain control. He wouldn't say anything except 'Let go of me, let go of me'. I would have let go of him, but he would have gone berserk. I started to shout as loudly as he was shouting. I said 'Vincent, look at the clock – it's nearly home time'. He eventually shut up, it took a long time to calm him down. It's never taken that long for him to come round. I normally get him when he's been at it [tantrum] for a good four, five or six minutes . . . He was going to bite me at one point, he didn't. I said to him if you bite me I'd bite you back. I said to him 'You kick me and I'd kick you back'. Anyway he couldn't, apart from the fact that I was gripping the child, I mean I'm 12 stone, which means I could control him physically. Eventually he calmed down a little, I then took him downstairs and slung him in my room and left him in the corner [of the room]. What I suppose he needed for his tantrum was to be put over my knee and be given a good smack on his bottom. Of course, if I were to do that the educational psychologists would say that violence encourages violence . . . But sometimes a good smack is what a child like Vincent needs, but now you're not allowed to hit the children what can you do . . . ?

A class teacher at Castle School expressed her feelings about an incident (observed by the researcher) involving a six-year old girl of mixed race origins, where she felt it necessary to use physical restraint . . .

I've been meaning to have a word with you about the incident on Friday, seeing the look of horror on your face [referring to the researcher] as I pinned Sharon down on the floor. I felt quite vulnerable. It made me realise just what we must be doing to the children and ourselves. Seeing the look of horror on your face, you being an outsider, disturbed me. But it is the only strategy we have in this school for coping with these children. Sharon had been sent downstairs because she had been difficult in class. Mrs R sent her downstairs. She refused to go downstairs . . . While I had Sharon on the floor I was trying to talk to her, trying to calm her down. It's the only way to control these children who are full of aggression and are regularly having tantrums

In private, a number of teachers expressed considerable concern about the use of physical restraint on children. However, partly out of loyalty to colleagues, they believed that this was the only measure that some children would respond to. One class teacher at Castle School admitted:

It's the physical restraints that we have to apply in order to control the children which is my main concern . . . Having to haul them out of the classroom before I can teach the others. Having to be so harsh to the children, it's just not me. I often think about it and it disturbs me, for in effect we are assaulting the children. But there is nothing else we can do. Children come to expect us to physically restrain them. I just feel that I have reached my limit with the school, but who's going to want to come and work in schools like this. What's worrying me is, teachers here who don't know what it is to teach in a normal school . . .

Teachers' use of physical restraint on children obviously cannot be condoned. If nothing else this act is illegal. Yet it would be crude simply to dismiss these teachers as 'bad' and racially prejudiced. As stated earlier in this chapter, the vast majority of teachers seemed committed to the ideals of equality of educational opportunity. Rather their responses can be judged on one hand as rooted in their apparent assumptions and expectations of the different groups of children, and on the other hand as a response to the demands of their job; which includes controlling children and establishing and maintaining order and discipline in the classroom (Hargreaves, 1975, Denscombe, 1980).

Fundamentally, the teachers' responses reflected what might be termed a 'survival threat' (Woods, 1979); Pollard (1980); Riseborough (1981). Essentially, the teachers' conception of themselves is as competent practising professional teachers. In order to 'survive', to avoid what Pollard (1980) terms 'personal and career bankruptcy', teachers, as with most other professional groups, must feel that they can perform their role adequately (or at the very least to an acceptable level of adequacy), and that there is a degree of congruence between the role they are required to perform. It is considered that few teachers could continue for long believing that they were total failures and that their perceptions of themselves were fundamentally at odds with the job they were expected to do. Of course, definitions of 'adequacy' (or unacceptable inadequacy) vary considerably.

Indeed, an individual's definition is significantly dependent on his/her conceptions of how the job should be performed, which is influenced by various background factors, such as training and socialisation into the occupational culture and the work context. It will inevitably depend on the extent to which the individuals are prepared to make compromises between their conception of how the job ought ideally to be performed and how it actually can be performed in practical circumstances, a state which Pollard (1980) terms the 'ideal-self/pragmatic-self tension'. Thus, where their survival is threatened teachers must develop strategies which allow them to perform, or allow them to believe that they perform, their roles adequately. In other words, congruence between their self-image and the nature of the role.

The responses of the teachers at the multiracial schools, therefore, seem to be compatible with the situations and processes associated with teachers experiencing a 'survival threat'. An additional point is that the presence of certain pupil groups, namely pupils of Afro-Caribbean origin, seems to compound the teachers' sense of personal vulnerability. Many teachers at the multiracial schools developed what Stebbins (1977) terms a 'custodial orientation' to classroom life, in which they placed 'emphasis on control at the expense of teaching', as revealed in this verbal report to a parent from a teacher in Castle School:

He's kept out of nearly all the fights (*turning to pupil*), haven't you? He's tried very hard when people were being naughty, he tried to come away, and that's not very easy, is it, when you're used to getting in there?

The school's sanctions system as control

So far I have concentrated on the pattern of classroom interaction observed between teachers and different pupil groups inside the multiracial classroom. There were marked differences observed in the quality of the relationships experienced by pupils of different ethnic background. For example, a negative relationship was observed to exist between pupils of Afro-Caribbean and Rastafarian backgrounds and their teachers. In the classroom both pupil groups were subjected to greater direction and control than their white and Asian classmates. Teachers' accounts of classroom events revealed that, unlike other pupil groups, Afro-Caribbean and Rastafarian boys were seen as potential threats to classroom management and considered to exhibit a challenge to authority in their behaviour. The teachers' perceptions of both pupil groups resulted in teachers exercising frequent control over the overt behaviour of these pupils. The strategies used by teachers in the exercising of control ranged from statements of displeasure to the occasional use of 'corporal punishment'.

The adverse classroom interaction observed between Afro-Caribbean and Rastafarian pupils and their teachers meant that it was not uncommon for both groups to encounter the school-wide disciplinary system. This section will now explore different pupil groups.

The work of interactionist sociologists (e.g. Becker, 1963; Matza, 1964, 1969; Hargreaves *et al.*, 1975) provides insight into the seeming inevitablity of the process by which some pupils became labelled as 'deviant'. For instance Becker (1963) identified several factors which may lead to the development of a 'deviant career'. Among the different factors identified, notably the most important potential influence is the reinforcement of negative judgements in subsequent interactions with actors in positions of institutional authority, such as police or teachers. Furthermore, it is conceivable that negative labels are likely to attain an even greater significance where they are no longer solely the preserve of isolated teacher–pupil relationships but carry the full force of the school-wide sanctions.

The schools of the study were found to operate a number of disciplinary measures. The measures ranged from the opportunity for any teacher to 'isolate' a pupil (for example, the child is told to stand in the corner of the room, or stand facing the wall, or stand in a part of the room away from the focus of activity), to the mechanisms for permanent exclusion from the school roll (expulsion). The former measures were observed to be frequently applied, carried little official weight and were rarely recorded by the school. The latter measure represented the most serious sanction which the schools (in conjunction with the LEA) could apply to a pupil. During the period of the study, however, very few pupils were permanently excluded for any obvious pattern to emerge concerning their ethnic origin. Between these extremes lay a variety of official sanctions, two of which were centrally recorded by the schools and whose application is examined. The first was the system of removal of the pupil from the class and the second was temporary and/or tactical suspension of the pupil from the school.

The withdrawal of a pupil from the classroom for an alleged 'deviant act' served the purpose of isolating the pupil. The pupil was required to work on a task in another class, or work out in the corridor or outside the Headteacher's office. The duration of the isolation ranged from a lesson to the whole school day, depending on the seriousness of the offence. The teacher was required to record the reason(s) for removing the pupil from the class. The parent or guardian was usually notified of the event. The importance of this measure of removing a pupil from the classroom is that it indicated that the pupil's behaviour was considered enough of a problem to warrant official action beyond informal word-of-mouth reporting.

Figure 2.1 presents the figures for pupils withdrawn from the classroom at Bridgeway, Castle and Dewry Schools during one term. The figures show that in all three schools white children are the smallest number removed from the classroom (Bridgeway 1.5%, Castle 2.5%, and Dewry 0.99% respectively) while Afro-Caribbean children (Bridgeway 7.6%, Castle 13% and Dewry 5.4%) occur in the

Figure 2.1 Individual pupils withdrawn from the classroom (autumn 1988/89)

School	Ethnic group	Gender	Age	Reasons for removal	No. of that ethnic group in the school	% rate of withdrawal
Bridgeway School	Afro-Caribbean	Male	5	Behaviour	79	7.6%
	Afro-Caribbean	Male	6	Behaviour		
	Afro-Caribbean	Male	7	Behaviour		
	Afro-Caribbean	Male	7	Behaviour		
	Afro-Caribbean	Male	7	Behaviour		
	Afro-Caribbean	Male	7	Behaviour		
	White	Male	7	Behaviour	131	1.5%
	White	Male	8	Behaviour		
Castle School	Afro-Caribbean	Male	4	Behaviour	54	13%
	Afro-Caribbean	Male	5	Behaviour		
	Afro-Caribbean	Male	7	Behaviour		
	Afro-Caribbean	Male	7	Behaviour		
	Afro-Caribbean	Male	6	Behaviour		
	Afro-Caribbean	Female	5	Behaviour		
	Afro-Caribbean	Female	6	Behaviour		
	White	Male	6	Behaviour	79	2.5%
	White	Male	8	Behaviour		
Dewry School	Afro-Caribbean	Male	11	Behaviour	37	5.4%
	Afro-Caribbean	Male	12	Behaviour		
	White	Male	11	Behaviour	111	0.99%

largest numbers. Given the relatively greater control and directive experienced by pupils of Afro-Caribbean origin, their proportionately greater representation in Figure 2.1 was in the predicted direction. Asian children, and girls in general (with exception of two girls of Afro-Caribbean origin at Castle) predictably do not feature in this table.

A further measure employed by Castle School for dealing with a pupil considered to be a disciplinary problem was the creation of a 'special class'. Children described as exhibiting very disturbed/disruptive behaviour were placed in a 'special class' staffed by a senior teacher. The pupils were withdrawn from their regular class for half the school day (normally in the afternoon), usually for a whole term. Both their regular class teacher and 'special class' teacher were required formally to monitor the behaviour of the pupils placed in this class. The importance of placing a pupil in the 'special class' was twofold. Firstly, it indicated that the pupil's behaviour was considered enough of a problem to necessitate segregation of the pupil on a regular basis from his or her classmates and regular teacher. Secondly, it represented a possible means of reinforcement of 'deviant' labels. In essence, being placed in a class designated for pupils considered to be of 'very disturbed/disruptive behaviour' means that the labelling process thus becomes complete, providing what Hargreaves (1976) called 'the escalator of deviance'.

Figure 2.2 represent the figures for one term at Castle School for children classified as exhibiting very disturbed/disruptive behaviour, and those who were subsequently placed in the 'special class'. The figure shows a disproportionately large number of Afro-Caribbean pupils (especially boys) classified as disruptive and in turn placed in a special class. The pattern here is not dissimilar from that which is well documented for their secondary counterparts (Tomlinson, 1981; Wright 1986).

The temporary withdrawal of a pupil from the school was also a measure applied with varying degrees of frequency by the schools. A suspension from school represented an extremely serious statement about the recipient's behaviour. A temporary suspension from school normally ranged between a day to a whole school week. When a pupil was suspended from school an explanatory letter was sent to the pupil's home. The parent or guardian was normally required to visit the school (to discuss the offending act commited by the pupil) before the pupil was allowed to return to school. At the time of the study, schools were required to inform both the school's governing body

Figure 2.2 Castle First School: Children classified as exhibiting disturbed/disruptive behaviour (academic year 1988/89)

(a) By gender and ethnicity

Ethnic group	Number of pupils	Gender	Number of that ethnic group in the school	% of that ethnic group
Afro-Caribbean	8	Boys	54	20.4%
Afro-Caribbean	3	Girls		
White	6	Boys	79	7.5%

(b) Individual pupils placed in a 'special class'

Ethnic group	Number of pupils	Reason	Gender	Number of that ethnic group in the school	% of that ethnic group
Afro-Caribbean	6	Behaviour	Boys	54	13%
Afro-Caribbean	1	Behaviour	Girl		
White	9	Behaviour 5			
		Behaviour 4	Boys	79	11%
		Behaviour and learning			

and the LEA of suspension exceeding one day. The LEA openly discouraged the use of suspension by primary schools as a disciplinary measure; a policy which the headteacher at Castle School clearly disagreed with. The headteacher felt that the LEA's policy merely served to frustrate the school's attempts to control those children considered to pose a disciplinary problem. As the headteacher explained:

We have decided that for children who misbehaved, we would only have them in the school for half a day. We have five children whom we had considered having in school for only half a day (each day). We were not allowed to do this, really we should exclude them, but the office wouldn't support this. I think because they are afraid that most of the children are black, and they can't really deal with that. Another reason is because the children are young.

Figure 2.3 represents a breakdown of the figures for temporary suspensions (by age, gender and ethnicity) for three of the study's schools. Suspensions appear to be a common practice at Castle School. Further, all but one of Castle School's suspensions represented tactical or unofficial suspensions. By contrast, suspension is a rare occurrence in both Bridgeway and Dewry. With respect to Castle, Afro-Caribbean pupils seem to feature disproportionately among the suspensions. This seems to lend further support to the impression, based upon observational and interview data and

Figure 2.3 Temporary suspensions exceeding a day, by gender, age and ethnicity (academic year 1987/8)

School	Ethnic group	Gender	Age	Reason for suspension	Number of that ethnic group in the school
Bridgeway School	Afro-Caribbean	Male	7	Behaviour	79
Castle School	Afro-Caribbean	Male	4	Behaviour (Unofficial)	54
	Afro-Caribbean	Male	5	Behaviour (Official)	
	Afro-Caribbean	Male	6	Behaviour (Unofficial)	
	Afro-Caribbean	Male	7	Behaviour (Unofficial)	
	Afro-Caribbean	Male	7	Behaviour (Unofficial)	
	Afro-Caribbean	Male	6	Behaviour (Unofficial)	
	Afro-Caribbean	Male	7	Behaviour (Unofficial)	
	Afro-Caribbean	Male	6	Behaviour (Unofficial)	
	Afro-Caribbean	Male	6	Behaviour (Unofficial)	
	White	Male	6	Behaviour (Unofficial)	79
	White	Male	7	Behaviour (Unofficial)	
	White	Male	8	Behaviour (Unofficial)	
Dewry School	Afro-Caribbean	Male	10	Behaviour (Official)	37
	Afro-Caribbean	Male	12	Behaviour (Official)	

Note 'Unofficial' refers to suspensions which were not reported to the LEA as required.

placement in 'special classes', that Afro-Caribbean pupils (especially boys) were subjected to greater surveillance, control and directive than their peers of other ethnic origins.

Unfortunately, the small numbers of pupils featured in the analysis of the schools' sanction system make it particularly difficult for any discernible pattern to emerge *concerning ethnic origin among the schools*. Yet it is possible to draw formative conclusions about different pupil groups' experience of the sanction system within the schools. Essentially, although pupils of other ethnic origins, particularly white boys, were subject to the same controls and surveillance as their Afro-Caribbean classmates, as a group Afro-Caribbean children experience greater negative sanctions in the multi-racial schools.

Multiracialism in the classroom

The chief purpose of the classroom is the delivery of the curriculum. In the preceding two decades, there have been considerable debates concerning the kind of curriculum which is appropriate for children growing up in a multi-ethnic society. The Swann Committee (1985) advocates that issues of cultural diversity and, to a lesser degree, combating racism should inform the curriculum. Further, the Committee insisted that multicultural education should form part of an education for all, irrespective of the location or ethnic composition of the schools. However, there is little consensus as to what 'multicultural education' means in terms of pedagogic practice. There is a tension between those who oppose the category 'anti-racist education' to the category 'multicultural education' (see, for example, Stone, 1981; Mullard, 1984; Sivanandan, 1985; Parekh, 1986; and Brandt, 1986). It may be a little misleading to represent these diffuse idealogies as mutually exclusive or implacably antagonistic (Leicester, 1986; Lynch, 1985), nonetheless, they clearly differ in tenor and emphasis.

Essentially, where multiculturalism, tends to emphasise the need for schools to reflect in their curriculum and practices the cultures of ethnic minorities, to overcome curricular ethnocentrism and to increase inter-group tolerance, 'anti-racism', on the other hand, stresses the need for schools to play a central role in combating forms of racism at an institutional and individual level. The anti-racist approach also advocates fundamental reappraisal of both the formal and hidden curriculum and insists that all schools teach about issues of racism and take steps to promote racial equality and justice.

The study's schools approach to the curriculum revealed an infusion closely aligned to the 'multicultural' perspective. The schools approach primarily emphasises cultural diversity, ethnic life styles and culture. The schools, without exception, attempted to promote cultural diversity in two distinctive ways. First, by offering a 'black studies' programme, on a weekly basis, to both Afro-Caribbean and Asian children; a programme for which white children could opt if they so desired. With the exception of Dewry school the 'black studies' programme was taught by 'cultural workers' (of Afro-Caribbean and Asian origins), who visited the schools for this purpose. Dewry school had a white peripatetic teacher attached to the school who, as part of her overall responsibility, taught the 'black studies' classes observed, which, with the exception of a few white children who had volunteered to attend, were attended mainly by Afro-Caribbean and Asian children. The classes involved the children in activities which ranged from visits (to the local mosque, cultural workshops, and exhibitions) to work on projects associated with festive celebrations (i.e. Dawali, Eid, Carnival, and so on). From both individual and group interviews with the children who attended the 'black studies' class, it was possible to obtain an account of the children's views on the 'black studies' programme, particularly in relation to the programme's content and its exclusivity. The views of the Afro-Caribbeans are summed up by this pupil at Dewry school:

LEANNE: We do lessons with Mrs A [peripatetic teacher]. We talk about Africa and the Caribbean. We talk about the culture of these people and saw some slides of Jamaica. We do things about Pakistan.

INTERVIEWER: Do you enjoy attending the lessons with Mrs A?

LEANNE: Yeah, I like doing the work, it's very interesting. It's about black people and I like that.

INTERVIEWER: Do you cover similar things, for example, about the Caribbean and black people in your regular lesson, with your class teacher?

LEANNE: No, that I can think of. We do that with Mrs A. Also this man called Joshu [a cultural worker] sometimes comes. He comes and tells us poems.

INTERVIEWER: Who else attends the lessons?

LEANNE: Pakistani children as well.

INTERVIEWER: How would you feel about doing the lessons which you do with Mrs A in your regular class, with your class teacher?

LEANNE: It would be good, all the children should do the things we do, not just the black, the Jamaicans and the Pakistanis.

The Asian children were similarly enthusiastic about the 'black studies' programme, but unlike their Afro-Caribbean classmates they expressed reservations about it being part of the regular class experience: As this pupil puts it:

SARBINA: When Mrs A takes us, we do work on Pakistan: The different festivals and that. Sometimes we do cooking . . . and we do things about the Caribbean.

INTERVIEWER: Do you enjoy the lessons with Mrs A?

SARBINA: Very much, it's interesting, she's been asking us if we would like to be in Pakistan.

INTERVIEWER: Would you like to do the lessons you do with Mrs A in your class with your class teacher?

SARBINA: I don't really know, because you know then the white people in class will start laughing and I don't like it, so Mrs A takes us in groups, all Asians in a group, and then we talk about it [Pakistani lifestyles and culture]. I don't like it when it's with all the class, because they [the white pupils] start laughing, and I don't like it.

INTERVIEWER: Why do the white children laugh?

SARBINA: Like you know if the teacher talks about Pakistan or even mention the word Pakistan, everybody start laughing and looking at my face. I don't like it.

INTERVIEWER: Is the teacher aware of this?

SARBINA: Yeah, and she tells them off. They start giggling.

This observation was shared by some of the Asian children's white classmates. As this pupil pointed out:

A lot of people, white people, start laughing when we do anything about Pakistan. I just ignore them. They talk about the Pakistanis, they're [the Pakistanis] just seen as something different. I can't explain. They're taken as something different...I say that you should just take them as normal people, as they come.

The few white children who attended the 'black studies' lessons found them a positive experience. Below a white pupil comments on his experience of the 'black studies' lessons:

ANDREW: She [the teacher] took us to a Caribbean school and got us involved in the carnival. It was very interesting. She reads Annancy stories [Caribbean folk tales]. She talks about Pakistan and the Caribbean all the time. That's what she's [the teacher] here for. Because she's always on about it. She's told us a lot about Caribbean and Pakistani. I enjoy it me, it's good.
INTERVIEWER: What's good about the lessons?
ANDREW: They're interesting, you're learning things, good things.

The second way in which the schools attempted to promote multicultural ideals was as a permeation in the mainstream curriculum. In all the schools individual teachers were observed to be genuinely trying to take the multicultural nature of the classroom into account in curriculum application. A common practice was to draw on the resources provided by the children themselves. Unfortunately, the teachers' efforts were not always immediately rewarded and their sincerity was often questioned by the ethnic minority children concerned. The teachers' efforts often only served to make the ethnic minority children feel awkward and embarrassed.

This situation was observed to occur for two fundamental reasons. First, the teachers often appeared to lack confidence, basic factual knowledge and understanding of the areas or the topic they were addressing. More significantly, the teachers also clearly communicated this lack of competence to the class. For instance, teachers frequently mispronounced words or names relevant to the appropriate area or topic. This frequently got laughter from white children, but floods of embarrassed giggles from the black children. This situation uinintentionally served to make topics or areas of knowledge associated with ethnic minority values and cultures appear exotic, novel, unimportant, esoteric or difficult. Moreover, the intended message of the teacher's aproach was often at variance with the black children's experience of racial intolerance in the school.

The black children's responses to the sincere intentions of individual teachers to use them as a resource were essentially to refuse publicly to co-operate with the teacher, dissolve into giggles or lower their heads with embarrassment, deny or conceal skills or knowledge. The white children, on the other hand, often laughed, ridiculed, taunted or looked on passively.

The lesson reported here, in a class of 10 year-olds at Dewry school, highlights aspects of this observation. As part of its language work, the class was looking at the linguistic composition of the school.

The teacher was using a text printed in two languages – Urdu and English – as a resource.

TEACHER:	Last time we talked a little about the different languages we speak at home and in school, and we made a list on the board, and I said that we would talk about this book that I found in the library (*holds up book to the class*). Rehana and Aftab might be able to help me. It is an unusual book. Can you tell me why?
WHITE GIRL:	It's got funny writing.
TEACHER:	It's written in two languages. English and . . . can you tell me, Rehana?
WHITE BOY:	Jamaican.
REHANA:	(*shyly*) Urdu.
TEACHER:	Is that how you say it? Urdeo? (*Rehana laughs, embarrassed. White pupils snigger.*)
TEACHER:	(*to Rehana*) Say it again.
REHANA:	Urdu.
TEACHER:	Urdeo. (*Asian pupils laugh, embarrassed.*)
TEACHER:	Say it again.
REHANA:	Urdu.
TEACHER:	(*mimicking Rehana but showing signs of defect in the pronunciation, laughs*) Urdeo
TEACHER:	(*laughingly*) How do you say it, Aftab? (*Aftab holds his head down, refuses to respond.*)
WHITE BOY:	It's Pakistani language.
TEACHER:	Can we write it on the board (*teacher writes the word 'Urdu' on the board*) because you see what we've been saying. We pronounce things differently. But not just to lots of other countries. We pronounce things a bit differently than everywhere else apart from Hillsfield City. Paula [white girl], where do you come from?
PAULA:	Portsmouth.
TEACHER:	How long have you been living in Hillsfield City?
PAULA:	Don't know.
TEACHER:	Since you were little. So Paula has lived most of her life in Hillsfield City but Paula's dad has lived most of his life in Portsmouth and all over the place. And he doesn't talk like me. He doesn't talk like Paula. He's got what we call an accent. A quite different accent. He pronounces lots of things quite differently. You are fortunate really, because lots of your teachers come from different parts of the country. I come from Hillsfield City. I've lived in Hillsfield City all my life, Mrs M comes from Hillsfield City, Miss R comes from Hillsfield City. I think that's it . . . I don't think any of the other teachers do. They come from all over the place, all over the country. When

you live in a different part, not just of the world, but England, you pick up different accents. Now an accent is when you pronounce words differently. One word that I would pronounce differently is 'Urdeo'. I know that 'Urdeo' is completely wrong (*looks over to the Asian pupils*). Is it spelt like that in Pakistan (*pointing to word 'Urdu' written on the board*).

REHANA: (*shyly*) No.

TEACHER: No, it's not spelt at all like that because that is not 'Urdeo' writing or (*with a grin*) 'Urdoo'. A lot of the things in the 'Urdeo', as we found a lot of things in Ancient Egypt, cannot be translated exactly, because there are some words that come in Egyptian, that we haven't got in English, some words in English that we haven't got in Egyptian, and there are some words in English that we haven't got in Arabic. That's why I told you that some parts of the Bible are quite difficult to translate because they were not written in English but...?

AFRO-CARIBBEAN
BOY: African.

WHITE BOY: Welsh.

TEACHER: (*laughing*) No, not Welsh.

WHITE GIRL: Jewish.

TEACHER: Arabic, originally written in Arabic. It can't be directly translated. It's the same with this book. This can't be directly translated. (*To Asian boy*) Can you read that? (*boy bows his head*) I think he's shy, that's fair enough. Well, I can't read it, I might even have it upside down, I don't know. (*To Asian girl*) Can you tell us about 'Urdeo', is it written like that (*pointing left to right*) or written like that (*pointing right to left*)?

REHANA: No, that way (*pointing right to left*)

WHITE PUPIL: Backwards.

TEACHER: It's written from right to left?

REHANA: Yes.

TEACHER: No, it's not backwards. It's English that's written backwards.

WHITE PUPILS: (*exasperated*) Is it?

TEACHER: Don't forget that when the ancient Egyptians and lots of Eastern countries were writing, we were still swinging in trees and living in holes in the ground.
(*Pupils laugh*)

TEACHER: And living in caves. We couldn't write, and they could write in hieroglyphics. The Egyptians wrote downwards. The Chinese write down from top to bottom. I'm not sure where, but I think there's somewhere which actually writes upwards, is it the Japanese? Bottom of the page to the top of the page. We wouldn't get Aftab to read this book because he's a little bit shy, I know he can read it...

It was evident from the Asian children's demeanour that they viewed their teacher's efforts to promote aspects of their culture in the curriculum with some reservation. Conversations with the Asian children suggest that part of this stemmed from the concern that to focus on aspects of their culture in the lesson merely provoked harassment and antagonised their white peers. The Asian children's response corroborated the findings of other research studies (e.g. Mac an Ghail, 1988) which also noted that black children feel embarrassed, even stigmatised, in such lessons.

Teacher perspectives

In this section the intention is to present an in-depth account of the teachers' perspectives on classroom life and their pupils as reflected in their verbal accounts and written records of children. Teachers' adaptation to the demands of the classroom has been discussed in detail above. For instance, the point was made that the circumstances in which teachers have to teach necessitate typifications (Woods, 1979). Individual children then become judged by how far they measure up to the general typification. The data presented above on the patterns of classroom interaction showed teacher and pupil relationships to be mediated by ethnicity. Teachers tended to treat Afro-Caribbean children (especially boys) in a more restrictive way than other pupil groups. By contrast Asian children were treated more favourably than their Afro-Caribbean peers, but frequently were treated less favourably than their white classmates. From the data, therefore, it would be reasonable to assume that ethnicity was a feature of teachers' typification of the 'ideal clients'.

It could be construed that teachers operate within what Figueroa (1984) termed 'the racial frame of reference', namely, 'a socially constructed, socially reproduced and the learned way of orienting with and towards others and the world' (Figueroa, 1984). To paraphrase Figueroa further, he points out that the 'racial frame of reference' provides those who share it with a rallying point for group loyalty and cohesion; 'the racial frame of reference' helps to bridge the worlds of a socially divided nation and to maintain its national unity against 'outsiders' (Figueroa, 1984). Furthermore, Figueroa makes the important point that 'the racial frame of reference' does not simply refer to a set of beliefs but is also informed by and significantly informs 'new actions', perception, judgements, thought, knowledge (Figueroa, 1984). Accordingly teachers' 'racial frame of reference' may shape their perspectives and the criteria for different-iating and classifying pupils.

All the views of schoolteachers in the study in relation to their experience of the classroom were concerned with the children's motivation and adjustment to the learning situation. Their views of the children's educability revealed extremely complex feelings. Often these revealed an ambivalence about their working conditions. Yet they generally exhibited personal and professional concern for the children.

The teachers' main concerns about classroom life related first to their perceptions of the children's competence and, second, to their behaviour in the classroom. The levels of competence across all groups of children were considered by the majority of the teachers to be relatively poor. But certain skills were recognised to be poorer in the white children, as this teacher from Castle School explained:

In all the groups, the speech, language, listening, the concentration, are low, generally at lack of competence levels. There are also low energy levels, tiredness, lassitude... poor responses to requests and a lack of compliance that goes across the board. If I were referring children for special needs, they would be more likely to be white. In fact, for language development they would be more likely to be white than Asian, because relatively speaking the Asians are making progress, given that you take into account that English is a second language. These children are more competent in English than the children who had been exposed to English... from English parents. That is when you really get worried, because you realise that the level of competence is deteriorating.

However, the majority of teachers, as this one from Adelle School, considered all the children positively disposed to most aspects of classwork:

Generally speaking the children do have, within limitations, a good attitude to work. They have limited concentration skills, but within those parameters they do actually do their best. Their attitude to work is one of 'I will do my best to do this'. I would say a child who doesn't try is fairly rarer than the ones who do... I think most of them have a strong desire to please and are also proud to please... They like the idea of doing their best, if you say, 'Would you like to try again?' If you don't make an issue of it, they will do it again.

Further probing showed that children were differentially categorised on the basis of their orientation to work. For instance, white girls and Asian children, particularly boys, were considered to be the most motivated groups. On the other hand Afro-Caribbean children were often considered to reveal the lowest motivation, a view expressed by the teacher below:

I would say that the Asian boys, in general, are the most individually motivated in that it seems to come from within, from whatever input they have had at home, but they are much more determined to succeed, they know their work and they listen, they have the greatest listening skills in my class and this is very generalised overall... The difference between white boys and Afro-Caribbean children is that there is no difference. If they have been to bed early, then they might do well that day. If something happened in the playground, they are not going to. They don't seem to have any incentive or deep urge to

44

want to succeed in that educational way that the Asian boys do...I do sometimes feel though, especially last year, that some of the children, Afro-Caribbean, felt like they were under-achieving and consequently because of that they wouldn't try. They would get to a point... where if they reached a problem like a stage in maths which they hadn't come across and they were stumped, they would get very upset about it, over the top, dramatic, upset about it, rather than just, 'I can't do this – how do you do it?' It was like 'I can't do it, because I am hopeless'. I had two children in particular last year who reacted in this way.

However, not all teachers felt that Afro-Caribbean pupils were under-performing in school. On the contrary, some teachers regarded the Afro-Caribbean pupils to be among the most academically able children. As the headteacher at Castle School remarked:

Believe it or not, in spite of the behaviour of the black children, their disruptive behaviour in school, this doesn't appear to be affecting their achievement. I watch this very carefully and according to our records they are mainly over-achieving, in fact, they are the most able group...They actually have a complete range of ability. In very general terms that group is articulate, linguistically advanced and used to conversing with adults.

Teachers regularly reported the prevalence of problem behaviour in the classroom and around the school. The problems commonly referred to by teachers were aggressiveness, disobedience, distractability, overactive behaviour, teasing, quarrelsome attitude, children being overdemanding, conflict with peers, having temper tantrums and emotional problems.

Boys were considered to be more of a problem than girls and Afro-Caribbean children were seen as being a greater problem than white. Asian children were less associated with behaviour problems. On the other hand, Afro-Caribbean boys were generally associated with aggressive, disobedient and distractable behaviour.

Teachers frequently talked about feeling worn down by the sheer number of teacher–pupil interactions which involved some element of control or response to acts of indiscipline, particularly on the part of the Afro-Caribbean children. Furthermore, teachers felt that a succession of disruptive moments in the classroom often led to a change in the nature of their interactions with the children. Thus a point articulated by a teacher:

I would say some days I fulfil virtually nothing. Quite seriously, some days it's a battle. Some days you are quite happy at the end of the day, I feel I have achieved quite a lot, it all depends really on the temperament of the children. And I mean the powerful children in the class, their temperaments really do dictate the mood of the class, which is quite sad in a school like this, 'cause it means that the new children and the quiet children get swallowed up, that worries me. They don't get the attention at the time that they should have.

These quiet children are likely to be girls, more girls than boys, but I do have some boys who will just get on with what they have to do and don't hassle me at all... I have one little Asian girl who I would like to spend more time with, because she has got a lot to offer, she just sits there and gets on with what she has to do and doesn't bother me at all. I think that is how they are brought up, don't you? To be quiet and get on with it, and they are not troublemakers at all, they are very nice children. They are swallowed up definitely, which is sad. Delroy and Vincent [two Afro-Caribbean boys] are the trouble, very disruptive. I have to admit I like Delroy, I don't think I would have survived if I hadn't liked him. I mean quite seriously as well, there is something very appealing about him. At times I could strangle him, he's a very nice boy, he's got a very nice nature, he's very kind. You get him on your own, you know, in the right place at the right time, he can be kind. Vincent, I have to be careful with because I find him very difficult to relate to. I mean possibly I could spend more time with them all, but at the moment I can't. I am afraid my attitude tends to be negative and I have to think 'Come on now, be positive'.

An examination of teachers' classroom logs[3], where daily experiences were recorded, showed a tendency for some teachers to direct their frustration at the Afro-Caribbean children. This was reflected through the nature of the teachers' written comments, which often ranged from negative stereotyping to insults. For example, this recording on Justin (age six), an Afro-Caribbean boy:

I think Robert [fellow pupil] may be in little pieces by the morning. He had an argument with Justin today and I've seldom seen a face like it on a little child. The temper, rage and marked aggression was quite frightening to see. I wouldn't be surprised in years to come if Justin wasn't capable of actually killing someone. When he smiles he could charm the birds off the trees, but when he's in a temper he is incapable of controlling himself. He has an extremely short fuse, is a real chauvinist and to cap it all he's got a persecution complex. He has to be handled with kid gloves.

A comment on the behaviour of Ruth (six years old), an Afro-Caribbean girl, was in similar vein:

What a thoroughly objectionable little bitch, she's intelligent enough to egg others on and seem totally innocent herself. She pinches, nips and uses her brain to impose her will on others. She's one of those children who can't bear others to have friends – she likes to break up friendships (and is very good at it). If she were to use her brain in the way a normal child would, she would be bright by any standards.

The teacher's rather virulent description of Ruth seems to show labelling of gender as well as a racial nature.

Not all the teachers' comments recorded in their classroom logs relating to Afro-Caribbean children were as harsh and intemperate in tone. Nonetheless, the illustrations presented were symptomatic of the feelings of some of the teachers. Overall, the teachers' views showed a general tendency to associate Afro-Caribbean children with behaviour problems.

As was found in relation to Afro-Caribbean children, teachers at the four schools often held generalised views of Asian children. Teachers in their general conversation, as well as in their interviews with me, often cited Asian children as a group being a 'pleasure to teach'. Further, there was a general feeling among teachers that Asian pupils were 'quiet' and certainly not 'troublesome'. This expectation is partly borne out by the fact that Asian children did not feature in the schools' disciplinary system. Yet, classroom observations indicated that not all Asian children experienced a good rapport with their teachers. In the classroom there appears to be a link between the Asian child's academic performance and the nature of the rapport experienced with the class teacher.

A point corroborated by the teachers' classroom logs. Indeed, the classroom logs revealed certain contradictions in teachers' attitudes to Asian children. Some teachers were less favourably disposed to those Asian children who were perceived as having learning problems arising out of language difficulties; those who were perceived as operating as an exclusive group; and those who tended to converse in their 'mother tongue' in the classroom. In general, teachers showed greater approval of those Asian children who were perceived to be socially integrated in the classroom and proficient in the English language.

School Transfer records provide further information on teachers' perspectives on the different pupil groups in the four schools. Before children transferred to their respective middle or secondary school, the feeder school was required to complete the Authority's primary record card for each child. The record card required the feeder school to provide information about the child's IQ scores, or reading ages, confidential medical and family data. In addition to the record card, the four schools were found to provide supplementary information on each child on transfer. The supplementary information provided by the schools consisted of a short description of each child which reflected teacher's opinion on the child's conduct, family circumstances, psychological and emotional state; and teacher's ratings of the child's ability. The Authority's record card and supplementary information were subsequently sent on to the transfer schools.

Figure 2.4 gives examples of the supplementary information on each pupil sent on to the transfer school by Bridgeway School. The information is in the format used by the school, except that each child's name has been replaced with ethnicity and gender. Both tables refer to members of one-year groups from Bridgeway School who were transferring to one particular middle school. The information in Figure 2.4(b) was prepared by the school at a slightly later date, explaining the slight discrepancies in pupil numbers. This was the result of changes in transfer intentions.

For Figure 2.4(a)–(b), several of the Afro-Caribbean children have positive comments and high grading for ability (i.e. 5 out of 9 comments; and 4 out of 7 considered to be of grade 'A' ability). On the other hand 6 out of 9 comments clearly imply behaviour problems. For all the other groups there are more positive comments or grading. Among the comments there are more references to special

---

Figure 2.4 Bridgeway First School; Transfer document

(a) Teachers' confidential comments on individual children (by ethnicity and gender)

	Ethnic group	Gender	Comments
1.	Afro-Caribbean	Male	Ability good. Roy's brother. Father came to parent's meeting. Potentially troublesome, keep away from T (no. 5).
2.	Afro-Caribbean	Male	Untidy but capable – racist mother.
3.	Afro-Caribbean	Male	Lazy but very capable. Aggressive. Support from mother – has been referred to psychologists.
4.	Afro-Caribbean	Male	Poor ability.
5.	Afro-Caribbean	Male	Very good, very disruptive, racist.* Attention seeking. Same mother as P.
6.	Afro-Caribbean	Male	Poor initial sounds, special needs – behaviour problem – three sheets to the wind (unstable).
7.	Afro-Caribbean	Male	Bright but lazy – can be a nuisance. Mr W taught mother. She came to parents meeting. Good.
8.	Afro-Caribbean	Male	Good ability – trouble and nuisance. Keeps running.
9.	Afro-Caribbean	Male	Very good ability, lively, silly, disruptive, not with Carly (no. 34).
10.	Afro-Caribbean	Female	Good ability, co-operative.
11.	Afro-Caribbean	Female	Poor, special needs, just begun to read.
12.	Afro-Caribbean	Female	Special needs – loopy – volcano mum. Hash†.
13.	Afro-Caribbean	Female	Able, seeks attention, potential, disruptive, disobedient, awkward.
14.	Afro-Caribbean	Female	Able, Paul's sister!?
15.	Afro-Caribbean	Female	Glasses, special needs, sulky, a bitch, disruptive, problem with mother.
16.	White	Male	Reasonable standard – needs pushing.
17.	White	Male	Nice lad but very timid – could need help, potentially disruptive if with bad ones.
18.	White	Male	Bright, but a bully.

19.	White	Male	Poor ability – special needs. Conscientious.
20.	White	Male	Good reader – attention seeking, a trouble. Poor at maths.
21.	White	Male	Poor ability – good potential. Keep away from Craig (no. 19). Can be trouble. Mother has a bad temper.
22.	White	Male	Good ability, bright but scatty.
23.	White	Male	Poor ability – can only add and subtract. Becoming cheeky.
24.	White	Male	Very poor but has potential – lazy? Maths/logical. Special needs involved – deteriorating.
25.	White	Male	Special needs – often late.
26.	White	Male	Work refusal – disruptive behaviour – educational psychology involvement.
27.	White	Male	Disturbed – maybe statemented – place found in special school, but Mrs F (headteacher) didn't agree.
28.	White	Male	Good but messy – parents have just split up.
29.	White	Female	Good ability. Father (step) is black. Confused identity [a comment on the identity of this pupil].
30.	White	Female	Good, James's sister.
31.	White	Female	Capable, but deteriorating. T's sister.
32.	White	Female	Fair ability.
33.	White	Female	Good, lovely.
34.	White	Female	Has calmed down. Good ability. Don't put with Gail (no. 14).
35.	Asian	Male	Good ability. Not to be placed with Paula (no. 29).
36.	Asian	Male	Very poor eyesight.
37.	Asian	Male	Special needs – has done link up.
38.	Asian	Male	Beginning to come on – ESL.
40.	Asian	Male	Special needs – struggling.
41.	Asian	Male	Good ability. Has time off.
42.	Asian	Male	Special needs – potentially good, insecure, bullied, co-operative. ESL.
43.	Asian	Female	Lovely – but suspected of stealing.
44.	Asian	Female	Language problems – desperately in need of help – emotional troubles.
45.	Asian	Female	Special needs.
46.	Asian	Female	Capable, nipper [a term for physical abuse – it is noted that this pupil is inclined to physically abuse others].
47.	Asian	Female	Whereabouts unknown.
48.	Iranian	Female	Very good ability, but only in country 18 months from Tehran. Contact Mr S [advisory teacher with special responsibility for these children].

Key
† This word underlined by the school referred to cannabis.
* The inference here is that this pupil exhibited attitude towards the white female teachers.

(b) Confidential ratings of children

	Ethnic group	Gender	(1) Ability			(2) Trouble	(3) Attitude			(4) Problem
			A	B	C		+	O	−	
1.	Afro-Caribbean	B		/		*	/			
2.	Afro-Caribbean	B		/		*	/			
3.	Afro-Caribbean	B		/		*	/			Psychologist +
4.	Afro-Caribbean	B		/		*	/			
5.	Afro-Caribbean	B			/	*	/			
6.	Afro-Caribbean	B		/			/			
7.	Afro-Caribbean	B		/		*	/			
8.	Afro-Caribbean	G			/		/			
9.	Afro-Caribbean	G			/	*	/			Psychologist +
10.	Afro-Caribbean	G			/		/			
11.	Afro-Caribbean	G		/		*	/			
12.	Afro-Caribbean	G			/		/			
13.	White	B		/				/		
14.	White	B		/				/		
15.	White	B			/	*	/			
16.	White	B		/				/		
17.	White	B			/	*	/			Psychologist + ?
18.	White	B		/		*	/			
19.	White	B		/				/		
20.	White	B		/				/		
21.	White	B		/			/			
22.	White	B		/			/			
23.	White	B			/	*	/			Psychologist + ?
24.	White	B			/	*	/			Psychologist + ?
25.	White	B	/						/	
26.	White	G	/				/			
27.	White	G	/				/			
28.	White	G	/				/			
29.	White	G	/				/			
30.	White	G		/			/			
31.	White	G	/				/			
32.	White	G	/				/			
33.	Asian	B	/				/			
34.	Asian	B		/			/			
35.	Asian	B		/				/		
36.	Asian	B	/				/			
37.	Asian	B		/			/			
38.	Asian	B		/			/			
39.	Asian	B	/					/		
40.	Asian	B		/				/		
41.	Asian	G		/		*	/			
42.	Asian	G		/			/			
43.	Asian	G		/				/		
44.	Asian	G	/				/			
45.	Iranian	G	/				/			

Key
(1) Refers to ability range: A = excellent well above average; B = average; C = below average.
(2) Refers to behaviour problems.
(3) Refers to range of attitudes: + = excellent/good; O = average; − = poor.
(4) Refers to children with perceived psychological problems and potential referrals to the educational psychologist.

needs, and fewer comments or grading indicating behaviour or attitudes difficulties. The teachers' written records (both the classroom logs and transfer information) are important for two reasons. Firstly, both teachers' classroom logs and the supplementary transfer information present a formalised version of their typifications of individuals; ostensibly, typifications which seem to be rooted in the ethnocentric assumptions or 'racial frame of reference' of the teachers. Secondly, regarding the written supplementary information on each child supplied to the transfer school by Bridgeway School, this practice reveals a process by which the reputation a child acquires in one school, can travel before the child to a new school or new classroom encounters. In essence, the information that the school passes on provides an opportunity whereby teachers 'learn about the behaviour and abilities of other children before actually meeting them' (Burgess, 1984).

Peer relationships

Another facet of daily life in classrooms is the relationship between children. Friends and peers are considered vital to children's school life (e.g. Willis, 1977; Corrigan, 1979). Indeed, it is recognised that children's social, emotional and intellectual development is heavily influenced by the world of peers (Sluckin, 1981; Pollard, 1985). Additionally, research evidence has identified factors which influence the formation of friendship groups in the classroom. They include academic ability (Jackson, 1968; Kutnick, 1988); gender (Stanworth, 1983; Clarricoates, 1987) and less conclusively, ethnicity (Davey, 1983; Milner, 1983; Tomlinson, 1983).

This section explores 'race' relations between children in multi-ethnic classrooms. It examines the extent to which ethnicity informs classroom based friendship.

Emerging evidence shows that children are 'racially aware' from an early age. Yet the view that 'young children are often unconscious of their colour differences' is still part of teachers' folklore. Over the past decade, despite obvious methodological shortcomings (see Cohen and Manion, 1983), research on inter-ethnic friendship patterns in multi-ethnic schools indicates that children do not appear to form inter-ethnic friendships to any great extent, rather tending to prefer their own group and displaying hostility towards children of other groups (Davey, 1983; Milner, 1983; Tomlinson, 1983; Aboud, 1988).

Where such studies have involved comparison of white children with ethnic minorities there have been clear differences between groups, with white children as young as three demonstrating higher degrees of ethnic intolerance than ethnic minority children. Indeed, in the nursery classes of the three nursery/first schools, children reflected their awareness of racial and ethnic differences in conversations with both teachers/carers and peers, and attributed value to these differences. A dialogue between Charlene, a three-year old Afro-Caribbean girl, and Tina, a four-year old white girl, during creative play in Castle School illustrates this perfectly.

CHARLENE: (*cuddling a black doll*) This is my baby.

TINA: I don't like it, it's funny. I like this one, (*holding a white doll*) it's my favourite. I don't like this one (*pointing to black doll*). Because you see I like Sarah, and I like white. You're my best friend though, your're brown.

CHARLENE: I don't like that one (*pointing to the white doll*).

TINA: You're brown, aren't you?

CHARLENE: I'm not brown, I'm black.

TINA: You're brown, but I'm white.

CHARLENE: No I'm not, I'm black and baby's black.

TINA: They call us white, my mummy calls me white, and you know my mummy calls you brown. When you come to visit if you want . . . She'll say 'hello brown person . . .' I like brown, not black. Michael Jackson was brown, he went a bit white.

Before an examination of peer groupings in the classrooms of the study's schools, it is worth mentioning the types of classroom organisation employed by the schools. As indicated above, classroom organisation has been shown to influence social relationships. Organisationally, the four schools employed a combination of multi-task and whole-class tasks in the classroom. The former arrangement involved children working on a variety of different tasks in a day. This arrangement increased the opportunities for children to interact freely in a variety of task situations. Multi-task activities encouraged children to choose classmates according to their interest in the task. Thus, it was not uncommon for children who were considered 'best friends' to do different tasks during the lesson, which often led to the shifting of friendship group membership. This arrangement was routinely employed in the nursery and the infant classrooms, and only occasionally in the middle school. The second type of classroom organisation employed by the schools involved the entire class working on the same subject or area of the curriculum. The lessons were generally conducted from the front of the classroom. Children were normally seated four to a table, and were allowed to choose their seatmates. The whole-class arrangement was routinely used by the middle school but seldom used in the nursery classroom. Both arrangements, therefore, allow children a choice and control over friendship and work groups. Of course, one arrangement allows considerably more choice and control than the other.

Yet classroom observations revealed both gender and 'race' differentiation. (Regarding gender groupings, as mentioned earlier in the chapter, Asian children, unlike other pupil groups, worked in mixed-sex groups in the classroom. An in-depth examination of gender is beyond the scope of the book.) Focusing on 'race relations' in the classroom, friendship and work groups show evidence of being affected by ethnic criteria. There were all-white friendship groups, inevitably so because – particularly in two of the schools, Adelle and Dewry – of the small proportion of black children. There were observations of white and Afro-Caribbean friendship and work groups in the classroom, particularly among the girls.

But, overall, observations suggest that, particularly among the white children, from nursery onwards, children showed a preference for members of their own ethnic group and a desire to mix, work and play with them rather than with others. This 'own-group' preference did on occasion reflect antipathy towards children of other skin colour or cultural groups.

The children's preference for members of their own racial/ethnic group is corroborated by an Afro-Caribbean Child Care Assistant at Bridgeway school:

The white children, particularly a set of white children, even though they relate to me and Tazeem [Asian carer] all right, they won't play with anyone else. I mean black or Asian children. There are a couple of black children that won't play with Asian children but they won't play with white children either. I've noticed that the Asian children play very well and they play well amongst themselves and alongside each other but they don't mix themselves as well . . . But I think there is an attitude in the school that makes the Asian children feel negative about themselves.

Even at this early age, white children tended to be extremely negative towards the Asian children in both their attitudes and behaviour. They often refused to work and play with them and frequently subjected them to threatening behaviour, name calling and hitting. An example of this is shown in the incident below in Bridgeway School.

A group of four white boys (aged three to four) were collaboratively building a tower block out of the building blocks. An Asian boy walked over with the thought of participating. Two of the boys were heard to say vehemently, 'No, Paki, no Paki'. Another boy pushed the Asian boy aggressively. The Asian boy wandered off looking quite dejected.

The nursery teachers/carers were also aware of similar incidents of this nature. As an Afro-Caribbean carer at Bridgeway School points out:

Peter... (the) blond headed boy, I notice that he used to go up to the Asian children in a really threatening way, just threatening behaviour. He wouldn't say anything. If the Asian children had anything he would take it off them. The Asian girls, they'd leave things, by just the way he looked at them. They'd leave something if they were playing with it. He would look at them and they would drop it.

In the classroom, white children engaged in persistent racist name-calling, teasing, jostling, intimidation, rejection and the occasional physical assault on black and ethnic minority children. Aspects of this behaviour are illustrated in the following incident from Adelle School.

I was in a classroom observing and working with a group of six white six-year olds on English language and number tasks. Taseem (an Asian girl) came over to the group, and with a rather desperate look on her face asked me: 'Miss Cecile, can you help me do times by?'

Taseem was working on a multiplication exercise which she did not fully understand. The ten sums she had completed for this exercise had been marked as incorrect by the teacher and she had been asked to do the exercise again. I spent some minutes explaining the exercise to Taseem. The children in the group were very resentful of the fact that I had switched my attention from them to Taseem and also that she had joined the group.

INTERVIEWER: (*after having finished explaining the exercise*) Taseem, do you understand how 'times by' works?
JANE: [a white girl] No, she won't understand, she's a Paki.
(Taseem is very upset by this comment and is on the verge of tears.)
INTERVIEWER: (*to Jane*) What do you mean?
JANE: Because she's a Paki.
(The other children in the group are sniggering.)
INTERVIEWER: And why shouldn't she understand multiplication because she is a Pakistani?
JANE: Because she's not over us and she's not in our culture.
MICHAEL: [a white boy] She's Paki! (*laughs*)
INTERVIEWER: What is our culture?
JANE: England.
INTERVIEWER: She is in England, she lives in England.

JANE:	Yeah, but she comes from Pakistani.
ALICE:	[a white girl] Yeah, Pakistani, she was born in Pakistan she means.
TASEEM:	(*dejected but in protestation*) I wasn't, I was born here.
JANE:	She couldn't understand, that's what I think, because she speaks Paki.
OTHER CHILDREN:	(*to Taseem*) Where were you born?
INTERVIEWER:	Yes, just because she speaks 'Pakistani' it does not mean that she can't understand how to multiply.
JANE:	Because when I say something, she doesn't know what I say. And when it were assembly they were doing a Paki dance.
INTERVIEWER:	Taseem was born in England, her parents are from Pakistan, but she was born in England.
TASEEM:	My parents are here.
	(The researcher continues to assist Taseem with her number work. The other children become increasingly resentful.)
JANE:	(*sharply*) Will you help me now?
	(Some of the children take to taunting and name calling Taseem. However, sensing my disapproval of their behaviour, they adopt a strategy of name calling by sounding out the letters.)
JANE:	P-a-k-e, P-a-k-e!
ALICE:	(*quietly spoken, but so I would hear*) She's a Paki!
INTERVIEWER:	What does P-a-k-e mean?
JANE:	(*with a mischievous grin, whispering*) She's a Paki!
TASEEM:	(*visibly distraught*) Miss, I want to go out to play.
	(Echoing of P-a-k-e from the other children.)
ALICE:	She's a Paki, that's what it means.

This episode is important for several reasons. Firstly, it not only highlights the existence of racists in the very young, but it also shows that the children are well aware of its taboo status. On recognising my displeasure with their remarks, they endeavoured to disguise their intent. Secondly, the children's behaviour provides an example of how aspects of the Asian children's culture made available to these children via the formal curriculum are incorporated and reworked in the white children's taunts and teasing.

The teachers, with only a few exceptions, mentioned that racial intolerance was prevalent among the children. Indeed, the white children's attitude and behaviour towards the Asian children was a concern for the majority of teachers. One strategy for avoiding expressions of racial intolerance was to separate children of different ethnic groups. The following teacher's comment was typical of many that were expressed to me:

I have to think very carefully when I select children to work together because, more often than not, white children will refuse to sit next to or work with a Pakistani. You have to bear this in mind so as to avoid any nastiness.

In their views of school, many of the white children volunteered particularly vehement feelings towards the Asian children. This example below from Dewry School illustrates the general view:

JASON: [white boy, age 12] I don't like the Pakistani children. I call them Pakis. Mostly Zahid, he's about the best one in the school

INTERVIEWER: Why do you not like the Pakistani children?

JASON: Don't know. Like blacks because I've got a lot of black friends. Most of me friends are black anyway. I've got more black friends than I have white.

INTERVIEWER: What have the Asian children done for you to dislike them?

JASON: Got me in trouble with the police, and that . . . They blame me for going in house . . . Saying that I've been smashing the windows and that.

INTERVIEWER: Did you?

JASON: (long pause, smirk) *No.*

INTERVIEWER: Do you think that it is really right for you to dislike people for no reasons?

JASON: (*defiantly*) Yes.

INTERVIEWER: What's right about it?

JASON: They're buying all shops and all that . . . There's only one shop what's in't a Paki shop round our way. And they're not going to let Pakis take it. Mr Smith round our way, he's white.

INTERVIEWER: How do you know he's not going to let this happen?

JASON: Because he's told me mum and that the rest of the shops been taken over by Pakis. it's not right for white people Everytime they walk into a shop they see a Paki.

INTERVIEWER: What's not right about it?

JASON: Don't know, I don't like it.

INTERVIEWER: Providing there are the things in the shop that you wish to buy, does it matter who owns it?

JASON: (*angry*) I don't go to Paki shops.

INTERVIEWER: It could be said that you're racially prejudiced?

JASON: If I'm prejudiced, I wouldn't like blacks at all, but I do like black. Some of me friends are black . . . there's no black shop owners on our road, they're all Pakis except for one.

It is interesting to note the complex nature of Jason's reasoning. On the one hand he expresses hostile attitudes towards Asians. At the same time he hastens to add that he cannot be considered 'racially prejudiced' because he has black friends.

Ostensibly, Jason's use of the apparently contradictory phrase 'I can't be prejudiced because some of my best friends are black' reflects everyday discourse. Fundamentally, Jason's rationale reflects the prominent interplay between school and wider society, thus adding credence to the claim that the 'fine-grained detail of school and class-room life' has to be interpreted in relation to the ideology of the wider society (Hargreaves, 1985).

The white children's attitude towards Asian children also extended to black adults. Many of the white children expressed a definite view against being taught by black teachers. My discussion with two young children in Bridgeway School, Samantha (aged seven) and Claire (aged six), encapsulates this view:

SAMANTHA: Ranjit is the best behaved [in the class].
INTERVIEWER: Why is she the best behaved?
SAMANTHA: Because she helps – she works here.
INTERVIEWER: Who is Ranjit?
CLAIRE: She's that lady.
SAMANTHA: She's that lady.
INTERVIEWER: Can you describe her to me?
SAMANTHA: She's got long black hair, she's got striped jumper on and she's got black eyes.
INTERVIEWER: And is she a teacher?
SAMANTHA: No, she helps Mrs M [class teacher], helps us.
INTERVIEWER: How do you know she's not a teacher?
SAMANTHA: Because she's not here all the time – she only comes Wednesday, Thursday and Friday mornings...
CLAIRE: ...and a little bit...
SAMANTHA: She's brown.
CLAIRE: She's yellower than Zahra [an Asian girl in the class].
INTERVIEWER: Have you ever been taught by a brown teacher?
SAMANTHA: No.
INTERVIEWER: Would you like to be taught by a brown teacher?
SAMANTHA: (aghast) No.
INTERVIEWER: No? Why?
CLAIRE: I don't like it.
INTERVIEWER: Why don't you like it?
CLAIRE: I just like talking with...I like talking with white teachers and (under her breath) I don't like talking in Paki's language.
SAMANTHA: In Urdu.
INTERVIEWER: Why don't you want to be taught by a brown teacher?
SAMANTHA: Because we don't like her because...she speaks Urdu.
INTERVIEWER: Why don't you like people speaking in Urdu?
SAMANTHA: Because Urdu people are from Pakistan and nobody knows what they're talking about...
CLAIRE: ...and we don't want to learn Urdu...
INTERVIEWER: So you don't want a brown teacher?
CLAIRE AND
SAMANTHA: (together) No!
SAMANTHA: I'd like a French teacher...
INTERVIEWER: You'd like a French teacher? Why would you like a French teacher?
SAMANTHA: So I could go to France when I grow up and I'd know the language...
INTERVIEWER: But wouldn't you like to go to Pakistan when you grow up?
CLAIRE AND
SAMANTHA (together, aghast) No way!
INTERVIEWER: No way? Why?

SAMANTHA: Because it's too far and I might get sunburnt because it's always sunny there and (*under her breath*) the people ... sometimes it doesn't sunshine ...

INTERVIEWER: You don't like the sun?

SAMANTHA: Sometimes I do.

INTERVIEWER: So you wouldn't like to have a brown teacher then?

CLAIRE AND
SAMANTHA: No.

INTERVIEWER: Don't you think a brown teacher would be a good teacher?

SAMANTHA: No.

INTERVIEWER: No? Why?

SAMANTHA: She is sometimes, but sometimes she'd speak in Urdu to the other children because some children like the Urdu and don't understand English and she'd speak in Urdu.

INTERVIEWER: And wouldn't you like her to do that?

SAMANTHA: No. Because we'd think she wasn't listening to us because she wasn't ...

CLAIRE: Because we'd think she's playing [not being serious with them].

The white children's assertion that they would not like to be taught by a black teacher, but would accept a 'French' teacher, seemingly overlooking the possibility that such a teacher might also be black, suggests a 'Eurocentrism' which is just as limiting ethnically as Anglocentrism.

Summary

In this chapter I have examined the pattern of classroom interaction experienced by both Afro-Caribbean and Asian children. Both Afro-Caribbean and Asian children faced negative teacher interaction in the classroom. In both cases this teacher response occurred when these children were seen by the teacher as an apparent threat to classroom management or teacher effectiveness.

Ostensibly, the Asian pupils (particularly the younger children) were perceived as a problem to teachers because of their limited cognitive skills, poor English language and poor social skills, and their inability to socialise within the classroom. However, there was also the assumption that Asian children were well-disciplined and hard working.

By contrast Afro-Caribbean children were considered to be disruptive in classroom. Consequently, they were always among the most criticised and controlled group in the classroom. Afro-Caribbean children were also likely to feature in the school's sanction system.

Observations of black children's relationships with classmates

58

revealed that Asian children experienced frequent racial harassment at the hands of their white peers.

Notes
1 'Gonah' is a term used by Muslims to mean sin (in the eyes of Allah).
2 Statementing is a formal assessment of a child's cognitive and behavioural development, normally undertaken by the school and the Psychological Service.
3 Classroom logs were used by teachers in all the schools in the survey as a systematic way of recording facts and incidents relating to pupils. They were available for consultation by other staff.

CHAPTER 3

Outside the Classroom

The child's experience of school is based not only on life in the classroom; relations with other children in play, with teachers and other adults in the life of the school as a whole, also help shape attitudes and expectations. Essentially, experiences in the playground, at meal times and in moving around the school are also part of the multicultural life of the child and the school. In essence, life does not stop outside the curriculum or at the classroom door. This chapter explains black children's interaction with the support staff and white peers outside the classroom.

Support staff: 'dinner ladies'

In addition to the teachers and the non-teaching staff who work in the classroom, in each school there were to be found female non-teaching staff associated with the schools' meal services – notably 'dinner ladies'. The staff working in this area were predominantly white and often had children who attended the school. The dinner ladies' main role is to supervise children during the 'lunch hour', at mealtime and in the playground. The four school lunch-times occupied sixteen per cent of the whole school day. During the lunch hour the dinner ladies assumed the role *in loco parentis* (because they had total responsibility for the children in their care during this period). Yet in terms of the school's hierarchy their position carried a low status and no formal training in working with large numbers of children. Few of them were observed to have any child management skills and yet they were expected to supervise and direct large numbers of children during mealtimes and in the playground.

The dinner ladies were observed to have a generally poor relationship with many of the children. That with the Afro-Caribbean children appeared to be particularly fraught.

Levi, an Afro-Caribbean boy (aged 6, at Castle School) describes his encounter with a dinner lady:

LEVI   Elene [white girl] said I go out with her, and I said I don't and she slapped me across me face... So I kicked her. Then Miss [dinner lady] slapped me across me face so I kicked her. And I had her hand mark on me face.

INTERVIEWER: Why did the dinner lady slap you across your face?

LEVI: Because I hit Elene... Elene said I go out with her and I said I don't. So she hit me. So I kicked her and Miss slapped me across me face, I had her hand mark across me face.

INTERVIEWER: What happened after that?

LEVI: Miss P. [headteacher] sent a letter home to me mum.

INTERVIEWER: What does your mum say?

LEVI: She's coming up this afternoon.

INTERVIEWER: Do you think that you should have kicked the dinner lady, was that the right thing to do?

LEVI: Yes.

INTERVIEWER: Are you sorry?

LEVI: No, I'm not sorry.

INTERVIEWER: Do you think that it is right that you should kick people?

LEVI: No.

INTERVIEWER: Then why are you not sorry for hitting the dinner lady?

LEVI: Because she hit me first.

INTERVIEWER: What happened when you went to see the headteacher?

LEVI: She talked to me and Mrs Harris [dinner lady] and she asked Miss [dinner lady] if she slapped me across me face, and she said she didn't... She said 'I didn't slap him across the face' because she didn't want to get done. And she did slap me across me face.

Individual teachers felt that the dinner ladies had a difficult task which was not always acknowledged by colleagues. But it was also felt that some of the dinner ladies expressed racial attitudes which were not altogether conducive to working with ethnic minority children. A teacher at Dewry School commented:

Dinner ladies don't really have a great relationship with kids or staff. They are not treated with any great respect by the staff. A lot of the staff don't even know their names. The dinner ladies that are out in the yard are great actually. Some of them have a hard time from some of the kids and, actually having said that they are great, I think perhaps I ought to make a few reservations. I think Mary, for example, while I would say, being a person with a heart of gold and all that, is a bit inclined to make these sweeping statements about them... particularly referring to black children. Yes, there is racism amongst the dinner ladies.

Racial harassment around the school

This section describes the lived experience of black children around the school, particularly within the vicinity of the playground. The last chapter has shown that children of Asian origin endured racial persecution in the classroom. They experienced regular taunts, teasing and racist name-calling by their white classmates. Both sexes were likely to be on the receiving end of the rejection perpetrated by white children of both sexes. This observation was confirmed by teachers' comments. Indeed, some teachers mentioned that such was the unpopularity of the Asian children among their white peers in the classroom, that when children were asked to take partners for an activity Asian children were seldom chosen.

Before we examine social relationships around the schools' confines, it is helpful to locate this phenomenon within the wider context of previous work on 'racial harassment' both inside and in the vicinity of the school; and on peer in school and playground culture. The Commission for Racial Equality (1987), defines racial harassment as:

> Violence which may be verbal or physical and which includes attacks on property and people, suffered by individuals because of their race, nationality, ethnic origins – when the **victim believes** that the perpetrator was acting on racial grounds and/or there is evidence of racism.

In the last decade several publications have emerged concerning incidence of racial attacks and racial harassment in school. The Swann Report represents one of the first publications to focus on this phenomenon. The Report in its comments on the experiences of black children in schools stated that it was:

> ... difficult for ethnic minority communities to have full confidence and trust in an institution which they see as simply ignoring or discussing what is in fact an ever present and all pervasive shadow over their everyday lives. (DES, 1985, p. 35).

Further, Swann recognised that the prevalence of racism was not confined to urban schools but was:

> ... particularly strong when [black children] are present in relatively small numbers in school and are thus less able to be mutually supportive in the face of racial abuse. (DES, 1985, p. 33)

Several studies have subsequently shown the involvement of young children in racist activity. For instance, Akhtar's study of predominantly white first and middle schools revealed that Asian children attending the schools were regularly subjected to racial abuse by their white peers (Akhtar and Stronach, 1986). In a survey *Learning in Terror* (CRE, 1988) a number of instances of racial harassment amongst primary school children were reported. The Burnage Report (1988) which was commissioned following the murder of Ahmed Igbal Ullah at Burnage High School revealed the most severe consequence of racial harassment. In association with the Burnage Report, a localised study carried out by Kelly and Cohn, *Racism in Schools – New Research Evidence* (1988), concluded that black children are most frequently picked out for racial abuse by their white peers in school.

By contrast, Smith and Tomlinson (1989), in their longitudinal study of multi-ethnic and predominantly white secondary schools, inferred from the comments of black parents and pupils (rather than by actual observations of social relations within the schools) that:

> In contrast to some of the public criticisms that have been made of multi-ethnic secondary schools and of teachers' attitudes towards black children, there is remarkably little criticism from parents that focuses on race relations matters. Just one per cent of parents mentioned racial attacks, or that black and white children don't get on . . . (1989, p. 62).

However, the picture of race relations in school typified by the majority of studies (that is the experience of racial harassment) is not confined to school children. For instance, a 1981 Home Office report stated that Asians were 50 times more likely than whites to be the victims of racially motivated attacks (Home Office, 1981; CRE, 1987).

A brief look at studies of child culture and relationship at school provides the necessary context for examining relationships between black and white children outside the classroom. Child culture forms at school partly in response to external factors (for example, the neighbourhood, social class and the ideology of the wider society), partly in response to school processes (for example, the official academic and organisational structures of the school). Studies of child culture have shown its sophistication and complexity (Sluckin, 1981; Opie and Opie, 1969). Child culture influences identities, belief and actions. The relationships between children can be seen as having three core elements: 'affect', 'inclusion' and 'power or status'. Affect can include sharing one's sweets on the one hand or dislike on the other. Children's relationships inevitably involve inclusion in some groups and exclusion from others. The group relationships can also involve an element of power as one group could dominate another, within groups individuals assert their interests at the expense of others. Furthermore, these social groupings frequently change with shifts in power between individuals.

Children carry with them their own models of the social group. These models are informed by ideologies derived from gender, race, class, age and how these come to constitute 'common sense'. The models influence social interaction and these models are continually shaped by interaction between children. Racism is one of the ideologies reproduced as children act with others in their daily life. It is through the family, school and neighbourhood that children develop meaningful ways of understanding daily life and how the cultures of children come to embody racism.

It was apparent from observations of playtime and discussions with children about playtime, within the four schools, that 'child culture' governed social interaction. Within all the schools, from six years onwards, children were particularly concerned with status and identity. In each school the qualities associated with high status were based on 'male culture'. These involved establishing a reputation as 'cock of the school', displaying physical and verbal aggression, playing specific games (for example, football), name-calling, particularly racist names. Name-calling was a means of asserting dominance and, since the most common type of name-calling referred to appearance, it had the obvious effect of marking out the boundaries with regard to identity.

Conversely, the qualities that were linked with low status, were concerned with being a member of a particular ethnic group, 'being soft' (not fighting back when hit), playing specific games (for example, cricket), and not dressing correctly (for example, not wearing the latest designer attire).

The child culture, however, reflected a number of contradictions and inconsistencies. For instance, the status hierarchy operating in each school served to exclude both girls and black children by various means. Girls were excluded from the male association whether in the form of games played or 'masculine' rituals which enhance male domination. Yet the peer group status accorded to girls displayed a version of the 'male culture'. This was particularly evident among Afro-Caribbean girls. Their assertion of a particular version of male identity was accomplished through acts of verbal dominance. Furthermore, Afro-Caribbean children managed to attract a reasonable status from most of the other pupil groups of both female and male which suggested that peer culture included varying responses to ethnic differences.

Nonetheless, at playtime, black children faced considerable and continuous racist abuse from some white children within the schools. However, the most overt racism was directed against the Asian children, a situation which was, in a very complex way, reinforced and maintained by 'child culture' in the school. Within the schools, racist attacks (both verbal and physical) were almost totally restricted to white–Asian children. The 'child culture' dictated that to be identified as Asian (or in the words of the children a 'Paki') was to be attributed the lowest status. Group pressure served to draw many children of other groups into incessantly having to re-affirm their own identity whilst at the same time denouncing that of their Asian peers.

The importance of identity to the children's attitude is reflected in Mustafa (a six-year-old boy of Italian and Arab origins at Castle School), his complaint about being mis-identified by the children as a Pakistani. Furthermore, he expresses the distress that this causes him when he says:

MUSTAFA: (*adamant*) I'm not Paki...I'm Arab...They keep saying I'm Paki but I'm not.
INTERVIEWER: Why don't you like being called Pakistani?
MUSTAFA: Cos they call me names.
INTERVIEWER: What names are those?
MUSTAFA: Paki, some, I don't like these names...
INTERVIEWER: Why don't you like to be called a Pakistani?
MUSTAFA: It's naughty.
INTERVIEWER: Why is it naughty?
MUSTAFA: Instead of calling you Pakistani, they could call you Banana Face...When them lot call us names, we tell Miss.
INTERVIEWER: You tell Miss and what does Miss do?
MUSTAFA: Sometimes she makes them stand by the wall.

As is evident from the child's remarks, Paki is a derogatory term for Asian children.

A discussion with two white boys, Paul and Richard (both seven years old) at Bridgeway School about languages spoken in the school and preferred language further illustrates why being Asian, or more specifically being Pakistani, symbolised a social identity that was generally rejected by other children:

INTERVIEWER: You both say that Urdu is one of the languages spoken in this school. Would you both like to be taught to speak Urdu?
PAUL: (*aghast*) No way!
INTERVIEWER: Why not?

PAUL:	Cause I'd feel shame.
RICHARD:	I wouldn't.
INTERVIEWER:	Why would you feel shamed?
PAUL:	Because everybody calls you 'Paki', I mean Pakistani (*laughs*).
INTERVIEWER:	What is so shameful about being called Pakistani?
RICHARD:	You get tormented.
PAUL:	I don't know but it's shame... everyone keeps hitting you.
RICHARD:	They think you're soft.
PAUL:	In the yard, they're [other children] always pick on just because they're not very hard.
RICHARD:	They [other children] pick on the Pakistan children.
PAUL:	And hit them
INTERVIEWER:	Which children do.
RICHARD:	The people who... (*pointing accusingly to Paul*).
PAUL:	(*interjecting*) And you do Richard.
RICHARD:	The naughty people in this school.
INTERVIEWER:	Who are the naughty people?
RICHARD:	Me and Paul.
INTERVIEWER:	Why do you both pick on the Pakistani children?
RICHARD:	Everybody do, 'cause they act clever because they can speak two languages.
PAUL:	Yeah everybody do, when your back's turned they always push you down. And when you go to hit 'em back they just run away.

The boys' comments highlight the attributes which contribute to Asian children being at the bottom of the children's social status hierarchy. Interestingly, for one of the boys, the Asian children's bilingualism was seen as both a source of weakness and dominance. Further, the comments suggested that Asians did not always passively accept the abuse which they received at the hands of the white children.

More specifically, the extracts above highlight the racial name-calling and racially motivated physical assault which flourished in the playground. This orientation revealed no apparent gender differenti-ation. However, racial fights did appear to increase with the pupil age group. For the Asian children, the playgound represented the epitome of school harassment. Rehana (an eight-year-old girl) at Bridgeway School talks about her experiences at playtime both inside and outside school.

REHANA:	I have been called 'Paki' when I'm like playing outside at home and in school... Some white boys call us [other friends] Paki, they get into a gang and start chasing us in the playground.
INTERVIEWER:	When this happens in school, do you tell the teachers about it?
REHANA:	Yeah, we have told the teachers about it. They [teachers] sometimes give them [perpetrators] punishment like telling them to stay in [detention at playtime] and after a few days they still do the same. After a while when they come back out [after end of detention period] they start causing trouble again.

INTERVIEWER: What do the teachers do?

REHANA: Nothing really. All the punishment they give is like staying in and doing maths or something. If they [the perpetrators] start hitting you again, it's the same punishment.

INTERVIEWER: Why do you think the white children hit and call you names?

REHANA: They probably don't like us.

INTERVIEWER: Why?

REHANA: Because they're always saying this is our [the perpetrators'] country and we shouldn't come here . . . They say that we should go back to Pakiland.

INTERVIEWER: Do you tell the teachers that the white children say these things?

REHANA: The teachers say that they [the perpetrators] shouldn't say these things, but after a while they [the white children] still say the same things again . . . I think sometimes that the teachers don't care what happens to us. And like if they [the white children] do something bad to us and the teachers don't take any notice, I feel bad because teachers don't listen to you . . . I don't think the school can do anything about it [racist name calling and physical abuse]. They've no respect for us.

Muset, a 12-year-old boy at Dewry School spoke in similar terms of incidents at school, when he described the day-to-day playground experience and forcibly expresses his disappointment at the response of many teachers to this situation:

INTERVIEWER: Are there normally fights in the playground between Pakistani children and white children?

MUSET: Yes, Miss.

INTERVIEWER: Why?

MUSET: They call us Pakis and hit us so we get mad and hit 'em . . . for calling us names and throwing our ball away.

INTERVIEWER: Do you tell the teachers about these fights and name-calling?

MUSET: Yes, teachers don't do nowt and so we fight them back and get their football and lose it. They [the teachers] don't do nowt. If we hit 'em [white children] they [teachers] say summat to us. If their colour hit us, Mr X [teacher] and Mrs Y [teacher] hit or mess about with us and we tell them white teachers, they don't do nowt. They like help their own colour. And when we hit somebody they [teachers] pick on us and make us stand near the wall [in the playground] and punish us if we hit the white people. And when the white people do summat to us the teachers don't do nowt, the white teachers don't pick on their own colour or the white people.

INTERVIEWER: Are you sure about that?

MUSET: Yes, Miss.

INTERVIEWER: Why do you think that the teachers do not tell off the white children, and yet they tell you off?

MUSET: They tell 'em off sometimes, but politely, but they shout at us [Pakistani children] and push us about and everything. But they tell the white people off politely and kind. And they [the teachers] shout at us.

INTERVIEWER: How does that make you feel?

MUSET: Bad, Miss. Teachers don't do nowt. Then what are teachers for?

What are teachers for, to stand in the playground just to drink a cup of coffee? My dad said that if anyone cause trouble with me, just hit 'em and don't be scared of the teachers.

The views expressed by the children in the two extracts represent views held by a number of the black children spoken to in each of the four schools. For instance, the acceptance that racial harassment was an unpleasant but inescapable side of school life, because of their colour and ethnic origins. Black children viewed the staff to be ineffective in their response to racist behaviour. Some children thought that staff's lack of actions showed on one hand that there was realistically little that the school could do about racial harassment, and on the other that the staff were biased against black children. In the latter case, not only did staff not deal with racist behaviour, they tended to blame black children more than white children. Finally, there's the view that it was legitimate to hit back to defend yourself against racial abuse. This strategy posed a dilemma for black children, since hitting or fighting was against the rule for each of the schools. The problem with hitting the offender is that this may lead to the black child getting into trouble with staff as a result, most likely through the person hit telling in order to get the black child into trouble. For many black children this dilemma was compounded by the advice from their parents (as we see for Muset) to respond to racial bullying by using the strategy of physical retaliation.

Two white boys (both eight-year olds at Castle School) were observed over lunch-time, name-calling and kicking out at Asian boys and girls. Both admitted to their behaviour and had this to say about their conduct.

STEVEN: (a smug smile on his face) I was doing it.
INTERVIEWER: Why?
STEVEN: Because I don't like them.
INTERVIEWER: Who were you calling names and hitting?
STEVEN: Every Paki in yard.
INTERVIEWER: Why?
PAUL: I don't like them, they pick on me.
STEVEN: (giggling) We're going to box them in.
PAUL: That's why I box them in, I call them Pakis.
INTERVIEWER: Do you think its nice and kind to hit people, other children?
STEVEN: (arrogantly) Yes.
INTERVIEWER: Why do you not like the Asian children?
STEVEN: I don't know. (paused in thought) It's the way they dress and speak. They speak in a horrible way.

Playgound racism does not go unobserved or without concern from many teachers. One teacher at Dewry School talked about her experience at break time:

There are many problems in the playground. We had the situation where two Asian girls were away from school for some time. One of them was ill, the other refused to come to school because she could not face being in the playground at break without the support of her friend. The Asian girls in particular at breaktime in the playground cluster around the stairs at the bottom of the yard, near the teacher, in order to protect themselves or safeguard against bullying by the other children.

A similar observation is recounted by a teacher at Adelle school, it is pointed out that:

The Asian children are getting so picked on, it's awful. In the playground the Asian girls never leave the teacher's side. We had one little girl last week, they [white children] never left her alone, she was really frightened. I mean she really did need protection... but we can't stand next to her all the time. Everytime I looked, somebody was at her.

Furthermore, the inter-racial conflicts observed in the playground were not always simply between white and Asian children. Often there were conflicts between white and other black groups. This occurred through the formation of gangs. Generally, two gangs existed in the playground, a white gang and a gang (composed of both Afro-Caribbean and Asian children) which often included girls amongst its members. The purposes of the gangs were to establish or make challenges for the position or status of 'cock of the school', in addition to providing protection for their members. Wesley an eight-year-old Afro-Caribbean boy at Bridgeway School explains:

WESLEY: We have a gang [in the playground] to defend ourselves.
INTERVIEWER: Why do you need to defend yourself?
WESLEY: Because you shouldn't just walk off and start crying... if somebody hurt you you have to defend yourself.
INTERVIEWER: Which gang are you in?
WESLEY: Desmond gang, black gang... there's a white gang, Peter's gang... We are the one who want to kick him in.
INTERVIEWER: Why?
WESLEY: Because he's naughty all the time. He calls us names.
INTERVIEWER: So there is a black and white gang?
WESLEY: Yes, black and white gang.
INTERVIEWER: Why?
WESLEY: Because we want to get so many people to get Peter. Do you know who's in Peter's gang? White people. We like having both, Paki, Jamaican and half-English and Chinese. We don't mind as long as we got more...
INTERVIEWER: Why do you have these gangs?
WESLEY: Because people hit people and kick on people's friends and that why we get in gangs, and that's Peter who kicks people in.

INTERVIEWER: And what do your gangs do?
WESLEY: Help people . . . stop people fighting and that.
INTERVIEWER: Do you know how they do that?
WESLEY: Get a few people. Right. If you see anybody hitting somebody, they walk over there and say 'Stop that'.

The headteachers and many teachers in all the schools acknowledged that racial intolerance among the children was part of the school's life. Yet there was sometimes a failure to appreciate the stress and distress of this experience of intolerance. A year head at Dewry School reprimands two Afro-Caribbean boys publicly for an alleged physical conflict with a white boy in the playground. Ten minutes into the lesson the teacher asked the two boys to stand by his desk at the front of the class.

TEACHER: (*in a hostile tone of voice, addressing the Afro-Caribbean boys*) Why did you hit Mark?
DELROY: Because he and his friends were calling us names.
TEACHER: I don't know them.
TEACHER: What names did they call you?
DELROY: Nigger and Black B.
TEACHER: (*hard, sarcastic laughter*) That's a good one, Black B. I'll tell you why you can't remember the names of those with him, because there wasn't anyone else involved. I'll tell you why you thumped him. Because he kicked your ball, because he thought it was his ball. Because he accidentally kicked your ball, you thumped him, that's it isn't it?
WINSTON: No.
TEACHER: (*shouting*) Don't tell me a pack of lies, about him swearing and calling you names.
WINSTON: He called me nigger.
TEACHER: (*called the white boy out to the front of the classroom*) Mark come here, did you?
MARK: No.
TEACHER: Go and sit down.
TEACHER: (*turning to the two Afro-Caribbean boys . . . shouting*) You're dafter than I thought. He's three years younger than you, and smaller than both of you. I could pick five big boys in the school and a couple of girls to deal with both of you. You're nothing but stupid little bullies and a pair of savages.
DELROY: He did call us nigger.
TEACHER: (*shouting*) I don't know why I don't believe you, it is something to do with that you don't know how to tell the truth.
WINSTON: He called me names.
TEACHER: (*shouting*) You can tell me until you're black and blue in the face, I don't believe you . . . Do you feel tough doing that? He's three years younger than you. He's been in the school for about six months. He's a first year. You think back or think forward. In a few months time when you're a first year or a second year at the secondary school you just put yourself in his place.

WINSTON: If somebody called me racist names, I would get somebody to beat them up.

TEACHER: (*a loud sarcastic laugh*) What a way of settling things, Winston. You know what to do, Mark, get your dad to come up and beat Winston up, then Winston will get his dad to come and beat your dad up, then you can get your uncle to come up and beat Winston's dad up, then when we finish we can have a war. Run around with guns . . . I really hope that when you go to secondary school there are some fifth formers and sixth formers up there that act like you two are doing down here. I know some fifth formers up at 'W' school that were here, perhaps I'll have a word with them . . . get them to call you a few names.

The teacher's intention, undoubtedly, is to show his disapproval of the boys' action and to underline the school's policy regarding fighting in school. Yet the teacher seems impervious to the concerns of the boys (for being subjected to racist name-calling). A response, perhaps, which is indicative of the school's perceptions of Afro-Caribbean boys (as identified in Chapter 2, some teachers considered Afro-Caribbean to be troublesome and disruptive).

A few white children in their discussions about 'dislikes about school' mentioned the frequently factionalised atmosphere at playtime. Specifically, they talked about the level of intolerance of a general racial or cultural nature which characterised social interaction between children at playtime and expressed particular concern about the Asian children. This feeling is illustrated by Thomas, a 12-year-old boy at Dewry School.

INTERVIEWER What sort of things do you dislike about school?

THOMAS: Bullies, there's bullies at this school that follow you about. Children not being friendly, being nasty.

INTERVIEWER: What do you mean by bullies at school?

THOMAS: Children bossing you about, if you don't play with them or in their gang, they'll box you [hit you] or something like that. I just think it's daft. You should go along with your own friends and ignore other people. Second year girls sing daft songs to the Pakistani children. Nasty songs, they run up to them [Pakistani children] and kick them . . .

INTERVIEWER: Do the white boys do this also?

THOMAS: Yeah, quite a lot of boys. Just about everyone bullies Pakistani children.

INTERVIEWER: Why does everyone bully the Pakistani children, as you say?

THOMAS: Don't know, because they're different I think. It's silly. Different like, different to us, don't eat the same things, they can't say certain words; they read the Koran and go to mosque. They [white children] say they come from Ethiopia . . . I think the whole thing bad and nasty . . . They [Asian children] tell the teachers, the teacher tells those [the perpetrators] that have done it off, but they [the white children] ignore the teachers, and carry on, some of the teachers ignore them [the perpetrators]. The Pakistani children ignore the people [the perpetrators] but they keep coming up, picking on them, and when they [the Asian children] are playing cricket they [the white children] take the ball off them [the Asian children] and throw it over the fence...After school sometimes there were fights in the park [away from the school premises]. I just think it's nasty, I take them [Asian children] as normal people.

Thus far, it has been shown that racist name-calling and attacks from white peers characterised the daily experience of black children, especially Asian children in the playground. Teachers were aware of the racial harassment experienced by Asian children in this setting. An obvious concern at this juncture, therefore, is to consider how each school responded to this situation. The school treated the racial intolerance that the Asian children experienced at the hands of white peers with varying degrees of seriousness. However, there was a common view expressed by the headteachers and teachers which, ironically, blamed the Asian children by pointing to a lack of integration or assimilation on their part:

I have children who refuse outright to actually hold hands with Asian children, particularly Julie [white girl] – she has consistently, from the time she came to school, been very specific about it. But she has also been prepared to say that the child concerned isn't very clean and so part of her reasoning is based on the cleanliness rather than just the racist thing. I think the teachers are concerned about it [racism]. Certainly we have had a lot of discussion about it and we have tried various means of attempting to integrate the children more. I think one of the problems with the Asian children is because they dress, differently, because they eat differently. They are also told, I think, not to mix particularly, that they are themselves rather a separatist group and so except in cases of children in general are not very open to attempts to see themselves as part of a larger whole, rather than as being children of Asian origin. They actually seem to see themselves quite specifically as being Asian children, as being Pakistani children. They do not seem to see themselves in any way as being children who happen to have Asian parents, they quite specifically see themselves as a different group.

The headteachers and many teachers also hastened to add that children's overt racial attitudes and behaviour were solely the influence of factors outside the school, particularly the home. As the deputy head of Bridgeway School asserted:

Of course, there is a great deal of racism in this area from the white family who can't get out, this is where the children get it from.

This teacher also expressed some sympathy for the white family:

I suppose I don't have to live among them [Asians and black people], having them living on top of you.

The responses of headteachers and teachers to racist incidents revealed an ambivalence not observed in their handling of other areas of pupils' 'unacceptable behaviour'. Where racist incidents involved name-calling few teachers refused to intervene. A common strategy, however, was to make a moral appeal to the pupils for tolerance and respect of cultural and racial differences. To single out individuals was considered to run the risk of exacerbating the situation. They felt it better to play down the incident itself and to make general and positive appeals for tolerance, as from the deputy head of Bridgeway School:

It's [racism in school] got much worse lately. Maybe it's just suddenly come out into the open, I don't know, I think it's a little bit infectious. You get one child who does it covertly and once that child is seen to do it and actually had a fairly devastating effect on the Asian children, other children who've got it in them to be rather of a bullying nature take it on. We decided we could really only deal with a small step at a time and we thought that we could positively correct it every time we heard it. From 'He's not a Paki, he's a Pakistani' and then get on to the more general unkindness of name calling. We found it very difficult to cope with because, in fact, calling somebody a Pakistani is not name-calling of the 'speccy-four-eyes' type and we were aware, as adults, that we were dodging the issue, but we couldn't think of any way of dealing with the issue except by referring to it as something that was unkind, was distressing for other people, that we didn't like to be called names and we felt, as a preliminary thing, it was better than doing nothing at all.

At Castle School 'dodging the issue' became counter productive. The inter-racial conflicts became so acute that the school had to write to the LEA asking for urgent support in handling the situation, as the headteacher explains:

Recently the school has seen an increase in the intolerance between our children. There is this racist undercurrent all the time. Not a single playtime goes by without an incident of some kind. There's several episodes of bullying among the children, in particular. I can think of a group of white boys who rush around the playground at playtime viciously attacking any Asian child in sight. Some of our Asian girls are terrified of going out to the playground at playtime. We are concerned that it is just a matter of time before a child is severely injured in the playground. As a school we seem to be having little success in containing the problem. I'm aware that what is happening in the school is a reflection of the tensions within the community, there's considerable racism between the different communities here. I recently wrote to the Office (LEA), basically asking for some assistance in dealing with this problem. You see as a staff I don't think we have the confidence or the expertise to deal with this problem.

The findings of the City Council's Report on Racial Harassment in the Education Service (mentioned in Chapter 1) corroborate the evidence presented in this chapter on black children's experience of racial harassment in education. The Report stated that almost one in five of those who had been harassed were children or teenagers. Much of this harassment takes place in and around schools and colleges. This harassment took the form of physical attack or incitement of others to behave in a racist way; offensive jokes and comments about someone's race; bullying, humiliating, patronising words or actions; racist graffiti and verbal abuse, and threats and refusal to cooperate with people of other racial group or nationality.

Further, the report considered schools' response to racial harassment, and found that among the schools there was 'a reluctance to acknowledge incidents of racial harassment'; and 'a failure to record incidents of it'.

Summary

This chapter has presented data on the interaction between black children and auxiliary staff, and white peers outside the parameters of the classroom. A conflictual relationship was found to exist between children of Afro-Caribbean origin and the lunch-time supervisory staff. The factors which lay behind this conflictual relationship were undoubtedly a reflection of the staff's attitudes and expectation but also a reflection of their lack of formal training in managing large numbers of young children. There was evidence of widespread racial harassment within the schools. The most overt racism was directed against the Asian children. This situation was, in a very complex way, reinforced and maintained by 'child culture' in the school. It was a culture by which white children marked themselves off from certain ethnic groups, and constructed a status hierarchy from which they excluded, for instance, the Asian children by various means. There was a sense in which this status hierarchy has a greater credence than anything that the Asian children could ever create as an alternative, simply because the status hierarchy both functions within the school (through its organisation, the curriculum and subject content) and is also expressed and authenticated by the macro-structure of the dominant culture in Britain.

CHAPTER 4

Parents–School Relations

Parents must assume some importance in our analysis of 'race-relations' within the four schools. As is apparent from the teachers' perspectives explored in Chapter 2, the home is seen as having a crucial role in influencing, if not determining, the educability of the children with whom the school has to deal. Such a view receives official endorsement by researchers who have explored the social roots of differential attainment (Douglas, 1964; Plowden, 1967; Bernstein, 1973). The central focus of this chapter is to examine teachers' encounters with white and black parents, and to explore the views of black and white parents on aspects of their children's schooling.

Parent–school relationships, like others, do not take place in a vacuum, and the context in which staff and parents meet play a crucial role in shaping both their perspectives and expectations. For instance, in the case of parents whose children are about to enter school, the parents will have some knowledge of the school, either from older children who have been pupils, or from parents of other children who attend the school and from the school's reputation locally.

The same kinds of influence operate on the teacher's knowledge of the community (catchment area served by the school). It may be based on real contact, as well developed school/community links, or largely on the reputation of the area and the kinds of parents who inhabit it.

Focusing on the issue of the schools' catchment areas, it was apparent from the teachers' comments that their perceptions of the catchment area served, and its influence on proceedings within the school, varied between the schools. Teachers at Adelle School did not see the school's catchment area as having a particular effect on what they were trying to achieve in the school. On the contrary, there were attempts to positively incorporate aspects of the children's backgrounds into the experience provided by the school. For instance, a sizeable proportion of the children's fathers were either miners or ex-coalminers. During the period of the study, one of the many themes covered by the whole school was 'coalmining'. This theme was covered from a wide range of curriculum areas (for example, the history of coal mining, geological and geographical aspects; mining communities and life styles and so on).

In contrast, many of the teachers and the headteacher in the multi-racial schools perceived the catchment area and the children's backgrounds as adversely affecting the school and what it attempted to achieve. There were constant references to perceived problems related to family structure and upheavals and criminality.

This teacher, at Dewry School, expresses a view commonly held by other teachers:

I don't think it is an altogether straight community. I think it is a part of town where there has always been a quite high level of prostitution, drugs and criminality, with some violence.

Many teachers, such as this one from Castle School, pointed to perceived changes in family structure:

I came across the waiting list for the nursery of ten years ago, and at that point we had to look for the names of the parents and whether the father was working and what he did, and when I actually took account of that, we had very few single parent families and particularly unsupported young mothers. In ten years that whole picture has changed radically, and in fact the large majority of our families in the old sense are probably the Asian community. And even amongst the whole community the unsupported mother is the norm rather than exception, which it was ten years ago. So it's a very short time for that sort of social change to have taken over, and therefore there are serious implications for the school.

The observation from the headteacher at Dewry School was:

Perhaps it's snobbish to say that a lot of the better families move away from the area.

Within the multi-racial schools, however, the ethnic minority support staff and a few white teachers frequently expressed concerns about what they considered to be their colleagues' unjustifiable negative perceptions of both the catchment area and the children.

The view of an Afro-Caribbean child care assistant at Bridgeway School illustrates this point:

It really annoys me when they [white teachers] keep saying 'these kind of children, from families round here' . . . 'what more do you expect' sort of thing. You regularly hear comments from the teachers. Children are children. If you give them the right environment I think they'll all make it. Rachel [white teacher] says it more than anybody. I mean what are 'these kind of children'? Wherever you go they're all children, whatever school . . . I don't think they [teachers] put a lot into it because they don't expect a lot. Like the head, what she said to me last week about the course [Teacher Training course]. She asked me if you get on a Teacher Training course, what kind of school would you like to work in? I said, 'an inner city school'. She said, 'why?'. I said, 'because this is where I'm coming from, and I've grown up in an inner city'. She said, 'well you won't get any gratification. I'm not trying to put you off, but it will be hard work'. So what's she telling me? That it's a waste of time? I told her that this is where I'm coming from and if I ever make a teacher, this is where I want to be. That just shows, doesn't it – their attitude, what chance is there for *'these children, these parents?'*

A major problem in interpreting what teachers say about the communities which they serve is assessing how well they really know, understand, and approach the values and perspectives of parents. The combination of observation data and teachers' views suggested that many of their views about parents were uninformed and based on negative stereotypes. In fact, some of the teachers themselves conceded that there was the need to create a greater understanding between home and school.

All the schools maintained that attempts to establish better relationships with the children's homes was part of 'good practice'. However, the schools were found to differ in their implementation of this ideal. The nursery schools devised special schemes to encourage both greater collaboration between school and parents and involvement of parents in their children's education. For example, there were Parent Workshops where parents assisted their child in the classroom. Parents were also used as helpers in the classes, particularly during art, craft and cookery sessions. Sometimes the parents withdrew groups of children from the class, for cookery or craftwork. Finally, parents were also encouraged to assist their children with reading at home through the 'paired reading' scheme. This scheme involved a child taking a reading book home once a week, and the parent listening to the child read, then the child returning the book to the school with parent's comments on the child's progress. Compared with white parents, Afro-Caribbean and Asian parents were found to only occasionally participate in initiatives which involved visiting the school.

By contrast, at Dewry School the kind of parental contact/involvement encouraged consisted of more formal invitations to the school to talk about their child's progress, and for special events (such as plays, concerts, exhibitions). From the sample of parents interviewed for this school, it was found that slightly more Asian and Afro-Caribbean parents said that they attended the formally organised occasions compared to white parents.

The majority of teachers and headteachers, particularly in the multi-racial schools, expressed dissatisfaction with the nature of home–school relations. Their view was that most parents were unsupportive of the schools' values, aims and perspective. A sizeable number of parents were even considered to be openly hostile to the school. A common view was expressed by the head of Castle School:

They don't come into school very much. They generally come in to complain. The parents don't care much about their kids, so you can't expect them to come into school or care about what we're doing. I don't think many of the parents value school work or value school other than it gets the children out of their hair for the day.

Interestingly, from the head's comment, it is evident that it had not occurred to her that the parents' reluctance, as she says, to visit the school, other than when there is a problem, may be a reflection of differing expectations rather than the parents' lack of care or disregard for their children's education. Indeed, many teachers blamed the home and the community for anti-authority attitudes and a disrespect for adults, which teachers felt many of the children displayed. As noted in the previous chapter, racial intolerance among the children was generally viewed as a reflection of factors outside school, particularly the home. Few teachers viewed the problem as related to school factors in any way. On the contrary, the view was that the schools had exceeded all conceivable options in their attempt to improve relations between children. This point was illustrated in comments from their teacher at Bridgeway School:

Asian children are called 'Pakis' and they don't like it. They are disliked by the children. So much positively is done to foster a good relationship between different cultures. Staff bend over backwards to foster good relationships. You're up against it because parents are set in their ways. They'll come in and say they don't want that 'Paki muck'. [Parents' response or comments on the school's multi-cultural curriculum.] So what can you expect from their children.

In order to gain some insight into parents' perspectives on parent–school relations, a sample of black and white parents was interviewed. The parents were asked questions which ranged from their involvement in their child's education and contacts with the school to their general satisfaction with the school. Below the responses of the different groups of parents are presented in turn.

Asian parents

Very few Asian parents participated in school-initiated activities. This low participation was partly because of language difficulties. The Asian parents almost without exception expressed considerable satisfaction with the schools. The parents particularly mentioned the progress that they felt their children had made in reading and writing in English. From their point of view, the school had been effective in these areas. This judgement, it appeared, stemmed from inferences made from the kinds of 'products' their children brought home from school and teachers' progress reports.

A parent of a child at Bridgeway School explained:

Teachers always say they work really well in the class, and the children always come home and say that they've done this and that. I'm satisfied with what they teach them in school in English. They do teach them up to the standard, I think. I have no complaint about the teachers. They are all good teachers.

Despite this approval, parents did mention specific areas that they were concerned about, the school curriculum, tensions between the home expectations and those of the school, and harassment of their children by other children in and outside the school.

The Asian parents without exception expressed concern about the lack of serious attention given to their children's culture in the schools. It was the view of the parents that the home was invariably left to provide for their children's 'cultural needs'. As a parent of a child at Bridgeway School stated:

We worry about the children, what they are taught in school. They learn about Western culture only and not about yourself and you come out not as a Pakistani. Parents are having to work much harder to find lots of time to teach them about our culture. The schools do have images of different culture, but the children, I don't think, are noticing. You as a parent might notice, but the children don't. We talk among ourselves that this is what we want, but we don't get the courage to go up and say to school what we really want our children to learn from the school, and what there should be. They should be taught Urdu, as well as English.

Parents felt that their confidence in approaching the school would be greatly enhanced by the presence of Asian teachers in the school. One parent with a child at Castle School said:

I would like to see Asian teachers in school, for the children to learn about our culture. For as much as white teachers can teach, they still can only teach them what they read in books. If we had Asian teachers our women could go to school more. They can talk to the teacher any problem. If Asian women can't speak English they can go and explain any problems to Asian teachers who could then tell the headmistress.

Asian parents expressed concern about the attitudes of the school on matters relating to the customs of the home. Parents felt that a 'clash' of expectations occurred between the home and the school, and that teachers tended to disregard, and were often not prepared to listen to, parents' views. A parent of a child at Bridgeway School explains:

I had some problems when me wife was ill. She went back for nearly two years, back to Pakistan...me big daughter, she was eleven...I didn't send her to school. And teacher came in our house. 'Why aren't you sending her?' I said I have to go shopping and all that. She said 'Well she's not old enough to look after kids'. I said that's right, but I'm in problem. If she doesn't look after them who's going to look after them? She said, 'That your problem, your own problem'. I said okay then you do what you like. She said, 'We're going to send you to court'. I said okay I'd like to go. After another teacher came and said 'When's your shopping day?' I said Friday. The reason for saying Friday, is because I don't want her to go swimming...[bit missing]...don't want to send her to swimming because the rest of the girls and boys go swimming...I go to the school and said my daughter can't go to swimming, because I'm Muslim. They said, 'well what about them [referring to other Asian children] ten girls there and they're going'. They [teachers] don't take notice of me...They said rest of girls go and they're Muslims, are you a special Muslim?'

Considerable concerns were expressed by Asian parents regarding the distress caused to them and their children by the constant harrass- ment from white children inside and outside school. Furthermore, parents were dissatisfied with the responses of the schools when this matter was brought to their attention by the parents. This parent of a child at Dewry School described a typical example:

Even though our children are older and live so near the school, I take them and collect them back from school. Because they're not safe. Because they get hit by other children. When I go to collect them the white children shout names and swear at us. My son in Dewry School, he has been bullied, somebody hit him and his glasses broke in the playground. I went to the headmaster and he said he would pay for the glasses. I said, you don't have to pay for the glasses. All they said to me is we'll sort it out. They do nothing. We say to our boy, 'Make friends with the boy, don't fight'.

When some Asian parents felt that Adelle School was failing to take appropriate action against harrassment, they removed their children from the school for a short time, as one explained:

My kids go to school. Kid says to teacher that other kids beat me up. They [teachers] wouldn't take notice. I keep my kids at home.

Despite their reservations, Asian parents were generally perceived by teachers to be more supportive of the school and its values, as one teacher at Dewry School asserted:

The first generation Asians are very very strict. In general they will come up to see the work and they'll say to you, beat my child, 'You beat my boy, you beat my girl'. They want homework for them every night if possible. 'If they don't work, if they're lazy beat them. I give you permission.' If I do I haven't got a leg to stand on. But they want me to know, I mean they rule them with a rod of iron. They're very disappointed, I mean very disappointed if their children don't achieve. I mean they're very very supportive, probably one of the most supportive parents we've got in this school. We have a few white supportive parents, but then we've got the parents who say you go to school because it's somewhere to go between 9 o'clock and 3 o'clock, and they're out of the way.

Afro-Caribbean parents

In contrast to the Asian parents, the Afro-Caribbean parents revealed a disillusionment with almost all aspects of their children's schooling. From their point of view the school was not adequately fulfilling the academic expectations which they had for their children. Consequently they felt that it was imperative to give academic assistance at home.

The greatest concern expressed, without exception, was the regular feedback which they received from school about their children's behaviour, being told that their child was, for example, aggressive, quarrelsome, unruly and disruptive.

This negative feedback led to parents frequently visiting the school, often with the aim of defending their children against teachers' judgements. This situation is aptly described by a parent's account of her experience of school. The sequence of events and feelings recounted are not dissimilar to those reported by other Afro-Caribbean parents.

Glenroy is five now, six in April and he used to go to the nursery and I had, I won't say I had as much bother as I had since he went to the big school, 'cause I mean he used to get up to that mischief and that you know like he was under table when I came to collect him at 3.00. But that weren't nought, that were just a little joke, but they like this . . . from nursery they used to ask something about that as well. Could I talk to him, you know, I mean, he was only four. Anyway he goes to the big school and he goes into Miss M's class and I started getting little complaints about he's being you know misbehaving, he's not listening to the teacher and he runs off and he doesn't come back when he is told to. I put up with that for how long, it's half term when they changed classrooms and he is in Miss L's class, and I put up with that for a good while, till he were five and were going on for at least about a good couple of months and from then, there was nothing but complaints. I was having to go and see Mrs D [headteacher] either after school or early morning about half nine in her office to talk about the same problem with Glenroy and about his behaviour and I thought of getting him into another school. I then thought I will give it another try and then he went in to see Miss L's class and then I were getting these reports. It was like they were wasting more time on writing the report than they were on teaching him. I know a few kids in his class who misbehave and I said to them [teachers and the headteacher] do other kids get these kind of reports from out of the classroom? 'No because none of them are like Glenroy!' So I asked them, what do you mean none of them are like Glenroy?' 'Well we can talk to other children. When we tell them to come here, they will come, Glenroy doesn't.' Well I know myself Glenroy is stubborn, he is very stubborn, but if something upsets him he will go off. I went to Mrs D's office. Something happened. They had had enough, so they asked me to see to arrange if I could come into school either in the morning and sit with him for a length of time or to come in the afternoon after dinner and sit with him, you know for an hour. So I did that. I said well the best thing for me to do was to come and sit in the morning. So I went in, I used to go and take him in school for 08.50, sit in his classroom till 09.30, 09.45, 10.00 and I noticed that I was still getting the complaints, after doing all of that. About well he was alright until I'd gone, and I just thought that me sitting there calming him all this time hadn't served no purpose so I stopped doing it 'cause I thought, well I'm wasting time and I'm still getting complaints. He is just five year old, they just don't handle it too well.

This parent described her dismay and distress when the school suggested that her son should be referred to the educational psychologist and at the same time the school decided to exclude her other child for bad behaviour:

She [the headteacher] said that Glenroy should go and see a psychiatrist. I said there's nothing wrong with Glenroy. What's wrong with Glenroy is your treatment of him . . . I went home and told the dad about it. He was fuming 'cause he's said we haven't got no nutter in our family . . . There's also problems with Judy [her daughter]. I were here [at home], we heard the knocking and I see this person at the door with her. I'm looking at her thinking an accident or something and I was shocked, really because the one incident that she got involved in they had brought her out of school. I mean I was under strain then myself, I were really depressed about it all and it were getting me down. I mean that school is enough to make you wanna get depressed, run off and leave your kids. It's all racism. I've mentioned it to her [headteacher] before.

Over half of the Afro-Caribbean parents interviewed had been invited to school on at least one occasion to talk about their child's behaviour. But over half had also made impromptu visits to the school after their child had complained about an incident involving a teacher.

This parent describes an incident between a teacher and her son at

Castle School, which led to him leaving the school premises without permission and returning home:

This is the third time that Donovan had come home to say that the teacher... had handled him in some rough way. Donovan even came back and showed me what the teacher did... she grabbed him by the neck. If he had been doing something in the playground or he was frightening somebody or whatever, she'd grab him and she would drag him like that [demonstrating the action] by the neck. This time he ran home and said that the teacher had pushed him down... pushed him back and he banged his head on the floor, and he grabbed his coat, ran out of the classroom and he came home. Nobody attempted to look after him. She didn't apologise. There was no recognition of what she had done. It was more or less, she did it and just carried on with whatever she was doing. I'm not saying he is no angel... but no way that somebody else is going to put their hand on my child except for me. If he's going to get punishment it's from me, nobody else. I sent up to school, I asked Miss W, the deputy head, if Donovan had been reported missing out of school and she goes 'no'. So I went straight up to the classroom and confronted her [the teacher]. She were stood talking to these boys and I asked Donovan's mates to tell me what happened right in front of her face.

Such confrontations with teachers in the classroom (sometimes during a lesson) occurred during the researcher's observation. In this case, at the end of the day at Bridgeway School, while the researcher was talking with a class teacher, an Afro-Caribbean mother, looking extremely angry, walked into the classroom with her son Carl (aged seven). Her son looked quite distressed. The parent stood just inside the classroom door with her son. The teacher was seated at her desk some five yards away. The teacher left her desk and walked over to the parent:

PARENT: (*in anger*) Can I have a word with you?
TEACHER: Ah yes. Me, do you want to see me?
PARENT: No, no, I won't be long. I want to know what's going on up here because I'm sick of my child, Carl, coming home from school, being upset all the time.
TEACHER: (*in an anxious voice*) Well it's a case of us all being upset Mrs K [the parent], I've actually prepared a letter to ask you to come to see me and talk about it. I've seen you before, obviously, on one occasion and it has developed even worse over these last two weeks.
PARENT: (*scepticism in her voice*) What's developed worse?
TEACHER: Everything. Workwise – if you want an illustration, this morning, Carl did not write a word until half-past eleven.
PARENT: And why was that?
TEACHER: No idea. He came late, obviously, and then he went to find out about his dinner, when he came back he said 'I haven't done anything over the weekend so I won't be able to write anything'.
PARENT: (*to her son in a sharp voice*) You said that Carl?
CARL: No, I said... I said I haven't got anything to write and then when Mrs C [deputy headteacher] came and I did it all.

TEACHER: You didn't. When Mrs C our other teacher took them and then you went, but you said to me that you didn't do anything at the weekend so there was nothing to write about. That was your reason when I said why haven't you started writing.

PARENT: And what was the other incident, I want to hear about that more because I'm sick to death of it.

TEACHER: Well it's the same thing, I mean, basically it's the non-working, it's the behaviour. He's so...

PARENT: (*interrupting the teacher*)...A lot of the time Carl gets blamed for things because he's black.

TEACHER: He doesn't get blamed...

PARENT: (*shouting at the teacher*) Yes he does.

TEACHER: (*very anxiously*) Yes he does get blamed for some of the things he doesn't do, a lot of the things he does do.

PARENT: Yes I know that, I know what he's like at home.

TEACHER: Yes, exactly. What worries me mostly is he's got a very good brain and he's not using it because he's being silly. And an illustration is today, when I wasn't looking at him, to make me look at him, he threw himself on the floor...

PARENT: (*turning to her son*) Did you do that Carl?

TEACHER: He always seems to want me to look at him.

PARENT: Did you throw yourself on the floor – don't tell no lies!

CARL: No, no, I was walking over there (*points to his desk*) to get my pencil and I took my pencil over there and went back to my work.

TEACHER: Well, I'm sorry, but if you ask the other children they will tell you the same.

PARENT: Carl, did you throw yourself on the floor?

CARL: (*tearful*) No.

TEACHER: I mean that's just one instance, there are many occasions of kicking and poking...He's not the only one, there are other children, but it's got to the point where he's stopping me doing my job. He is being very rude and cheeky all the time and I had to tell him five times to move.

PARENT: Why wouldn't you move Carl?

CARL: I was getting on with my work and I wanted to sit where I was.

TEACHER: Like I said, kicking everything on the floor and around the floor – disturbing other people working. It gets to the point where – he wasn't in this morning as you know...

PARENT: I know because he got up late.

TEACHER: For the first half-hour my kids were very quiet and everyone got on very well, but the difference when Carl came in, you wouldn't believe it. It's, you know, I'm having to nag all the time, shout at him all the time and it gets very wearing – for him to listen to me and for me to keep on.

PARENT: The best thing for me to do then is to move him from this school isn't it?

TEACHER: I don't think taking him away from school is the answer because it's his relationship with the teachers and children...

PARENT: (*in anger*) Well I mean your lot's sick of him, you told me that, you said you're sick of him, and even though you're sick of him you shouldn't say that...you're sick of him, the other teachers are sick of him...

TEACHER: (*in anger*) Well we are sick of him, sick of telling him...

PARENT: Well you shouldn't say things like that to a seven-year-old!

TEACHER: (*turning to Carl*) You know what we mean, I think, don't you Carl? You understand? As I say he's clever enough, but if you have somebody on at you all the time when you've got 20 other children wanting you to look at them all the time, poking people, bullying people, in trouble with the other teachers, can't sit in the hall so the other teachers send him out, it's happening all the time, every minute there's something...

PARENT: Well that's it then, I'll have to move him if your lot's sick of him...I've been up to this school dozens of times over Carl's behaviour. Carl's done this, Carl's done that, he gets blamed for things – I'm not saying he doesn't do it, because I know what Carl's like at home, but a lot of things he gets blamed for it's just because he's bad or it's just because he doesn't know – some things happen he says, like – he says everybody turns round and says Miss, Carl did this and because he's seen as bad, he gets blamed for it and it's the same with the dinner ladies.

TEACHER: (*defensively*) Yes, yes, the trouble is you see, you get that – that's right – that does happen, all right, because you get...he does get the blame for things.

PARENT: (*shouting*) Well what you ought to do is find out who's in the wrong.

TEACHER: Well yes, we do sometimes.

PARENT: Instead of blaming him all the time. He gets blamed for a lot of things what he's not done. I know what Carl is capable of doing...I still think it might be better if he didn't know nobody, then he might start from scratch because when you first went to a new school you don't know anybody so you're forced to be quiet isn't it?

TEACHER: Well, I mean I don't know that, I can't say because that depends on the individual settling down in school and how he then solves his relationships. I know he's got one or two very good friends and then the next minute you find that he hits something or they've done something to him – and he is always telling tales – you know, somebody's done this, somebody's done that.

PARENT: I know Carl tells tales, I know what sort of tales he tells. He don't tell lies not only for you – when he breaks something at home he'll say he didn't do it because he knows he'll get hit for it.

TEACHER: Well you see the problem is I don't know where I go from here, because telling him off just doesn't stop him as far as I'm concerned, because he won't do as he's told, at least not the first time and I have to say things so many times – it's not only bad for him, it's bad for the rest of the class and it's got to the point now, as I say, where I'm not able to do my job properly.

PARENT: Because of him?

TEACHER: Because of all the things I have to tell him and re-tell him.

PARENT: No, it's wrong...I'm just going to have to move him then, so you can get on with your work isn't it?

TEACHER: Well that's not necessarily the answer, the answer is for him to change and to agree to work in the classroom.

PARENT: I've talked to him loads and loads of times and I can't change him.

TEACHER: Well I had a good word with him on two nights last week, when we had two bad days, and he seems very reasonable until he comes in next day. Very reasonable. As I say it's a difficult problem and I knew there would be no answer. I'm just very worried for him because he understands the difficulties as well and he knows which is right and which is wrong. I mean when he's doing something he knows what he should be doing. When Carl's done something wrong and he's told off, very reasonably, about it then you get, you know, this sulky look and he'll go and sit down and sulk when he deserves a correction, but he doesn't think that's fair. If I gave him a good push that would be terrible, but you see he's quite prepared to give other peopie a good push and then it's not fair when he's told off.

PARENT: When Carl's done wrong, he doesn't come home and tell me nothing – when he's right he always comes home and tells me – like one day last week, I think, he said one of the lads in here called you (to Carl) what?

CARL: A nigger.

PARENT: And he got into trouble for that which I don't think that was right. You shouldn't have kids going around saying things like that.

TEACHER: No, that's true.

CARL: I was sitting outside the staffroom at breaktime because I got into trouble, and Lee [white pupil] call me a nigger and I hit him.

TEACHER: Well I mean the thing is, it's obvious, he should have come straight away and said something instead of doing the hitting.

PARENT: Yes but you're not going to do nothing . . . well anyway you not do nothing about it.

TEACHER Oh yes I do.

PARENT: And because you think Carl is bad you just ignore him – you do!

TEACHER: No! If somebody else did the same thing they would be told off in the same way, but they don't do the same things.

PARENT: Well I've told him, anybody calls him names – black names – hit 'em and I've told him if anybody hits you at school and you don't hit 'em first, hit 'em back. That's what my Mum told me when I was growing up.

TEACHER: But that doesn't help the school does it?

PARENT: And it's no good telling the teachers because they don't do nothing about it.

TEACHER: We do something at the time, if we see it happening, certainly.

PARENT: It's like quite a few times when I used to come up here before, somebody's hit him and he's turned round and hit 'em back. The teachers didn't see when the other white kids hit him and Carl gets into trouble for it.

TEACHER: Well, I mean, yes, sometimes that does happen.

PARENT: And he's told them that it was them [white children] that was hitting him but they [teachers] took no notice because he's black. Carl's always getting this, Carl's always hitting somebody, Carl's always doing something, pushing somebody.

TEACHER: Then I'm sorry about that, but four or five times in a day he's done something wrong and how many times does he come home and tell you when he's done wrong?

PARENT: No, when he's wrong he never tells me nothing but when he's right he comes home and he tells me.

TEACHER: Yes, but how many times is that?

PARENT: We're going downstairs to see Mrs J [headteacher], about it, come on Carl . . .
(*Parent storms out of the room banging the door behind her.*)

TEACHER: (*to the researcher*) Well you see this is what we face all the time. He doesn't tell lies!

The tendency for Afro-Caribbean parents to enter the classroom and engage in open confrontation with the teacher frequently led to a worsening relationship from which it was difficult for either the teacher or the parent to extricate themselves.

This pattern of visiting the school to complain, and the confrontations which frequently followed, led teachers and headteachers to consider Afro-Caribbean parents to be generally hostile to the school. They were also perceived as having total disregard for the headteacher and teachers' authority, and to be aggressive and threatening. The headteacher at Adelle School explained:

Well I have a couple of Caribbean mothers who are very volatile, I think I would describe it as that. You don't know how they are going to react to something and obviously you have to try and be as positive as you can. I will give you an example. We have just started self assessment, children's self assessment folders, and prior to that I discussed it with the Governors; explained what it was going to be and they were full of enthusiasm for the idea – they thought it was great so I called a parents' meeting. Now obviously, at the time of day, of course, it meant that some parents could not be there, but we sent home a written statement explaining what it was about so that they had some indication and we explained that the whole thing was very positive. The children were allowed to put into their folders whatever they wanted – it was their choice. The reason that they wanted to put it in was written on the piece of work or picture or whatever, so that the folder would go home once a term and the parents were asked to discuss it with the children, comment on it and if they wish to, write a comment on it describing things that went off at home, interests, activity, where they went with the children etc. They didn't have to do it, but they could if they wanted to. Now most of the parents returned some comment, and some of them were really moving. I mean it really brought tears to your eyes, honestly, and the benefit was enormous. You know, I mean the kids were so proud of these folders and I'd say it has got such a good response that they have decided to do it right through the school, except for this one child. This Afro-Caribbean child, whose mother came in and threatened to do the teacher over, was very aggressive, said that the folder was rubbish, that we taught her children absolutely nothing. He has just been wasting his time here. We weren't fit to be teachers and bla bla bla... you see... and really upset the two teachers concerned because this child had been here a year and a half in the school and been through the nurture unit [nursery] and really worked hard... a lovely child, and obviously it was very upsetting. It can be very distressing for the teacher to have all this going on. You know, especially the physical threats, that she was going to get her husband to come and bash her up and all this business and really really awful. So anyway I came in the next day and there she was waiting for me [the parent]. I think she came in in the afternoon, ready to duff me up as well. I spent about one hour and a half trying to explain things to her and calm her down. And in actual fact things have improved a bit now. But you never know when she is going to go off again. You are always living with that particular sort of behaviour. Now this child can be naughty at times, but it comes from this whole business of this volatile relationship that she has with her own child, you know.

Essentially, all the headteachers without exception considered the majority of Afro-Caribbean parents to be a problem, with a tendency to be anxious about their children's academic progress. Not every headteacher disregarded the parents' views. It was occasionally admitted that perhaps the schools had not done enough to obtain the trust of the black parents. As the headteacher at Castle School remarked:

The black parents tend to be quite articulate, intelligent and very keen on their children's education. The sorts of conversations I have with a lot of the black parents are very different to the ones I have with white parents. I have a large group of white parents with very low levels of intellectual functioning. But they [black parents] have an attitude to authority. And the saddest thing is I don't think that we've actually done enough to get their trust. I'm still a headteacher, a white headteacher. They can go away quite pleased if they came and I agree with what they want. But if I don't, I'm back to being white authority again. It's that barrier really, institutional racism, call it what you will.

In a study of inner-city primary schools Tizard *et al.* (1988) found that answers given by teachers to the question 'What has been your experience of West Indian parents?' revealed that a number of teachers had stereotypes of these parents, with only 13 per cent refraining from offering generalisations. Seventy per cent offered negative evaluations, asserting, for example, that West Indian parents were too concerned about their children's education, expected too high a standard of achievement, and were too authoritarian at home. However, about one-third of the teachers gave positive evaluations of West Indian parents, some of these similar to the characteristics evaluated as negative by others, such as keen on education.

Overall, the comments of the Afro-Caribbean parents revealed considerable unhappiness with their children's schooling; a feeling which ostensibly gave rise to despair and frustration. An added contribution to these parents' perspective, perhaps, was their own experience of schooling in Britain which, according to the parents, was characterised by poor relations with their teachers. Many of the Afro-Caribbean parents expressed disbelief that the situation had changed much in 15–20 years since their own experience of schooling. A point expressed in this parent's comment:

I hated school, simply because every day we were called black bastard, black this, black that. The teachers picked on us, thought we had no brains. I just get the feeling that they are not giving the black kid a fair chance or goal. It is not as if you hear any great 'Oh yes we have to do this'. But it doesn't just happen, you can't blame the secondary teachers for that. It starts from the infant school. It really does. You have to be there for a day, a whole day, a whole month. You are sitting and watching it start from then. The stereotyping, the labelling, the pigeon-holing, and then that kid takes it all the way up. Then the problem starts there then it just mounts up, it really does. It is the attitudes of the teachers ... I mean you know that prejudices exist in the community, it is bound to be in the school. So then you come to the conclusion that you can't get away from it, it is about time if we understand it, that we find a way to fight it.

White parents

The white parents generally expressed satisfaction with the school. From their point of view, the school's ability to transmit skills of reading, writing and numeracy was an important measure of its effectiveness. However, parents considered their children being 'happy in school' as equally important, if not vital, as in this view expressed by one parent of a child at Adelle School:

They are very happy children here. Like most parents, providing the kids are happy at school, you are quite glad to send them there. I think learning comes secondary to a lot of people. Who wants their child screaming every day because they don't want to go to school? I have never heard my children once say that they didn't want to come to school and that is what counts for me.

Nearly half of these parents had been participating in schools activities such as Parent Workshops, mainly to be able to assess their child's progress. As a parent of a child in Adelle School remarked:

I think when you do come into school and work with a group of children, you can judge how well your child is doing by how well the others are doing. You can tell whether they are up to scratch or you know if they're lagging behind a little.

Conversely, the few parents who had not participated in the school-initiated activities, had not done so because, in the words of one parent of a child at Bridgeway School:

They are inviting parents to come into school too much. I don't agree with that. I think the teacher is qualified to do more than what a parent should. A parent should do it at home – got plenty of time to do it at home. It is up to the teacher. Not that I wouldn't help, but I do think if I was clever enough to teach my child I would have been a teacher. To me teachers are supposed to be cleverer than me. They were when I went to school. Peter had done two years there and they always say – you can come any time. The doors are always open but I don't think that you should put your nose in – that's what I think. You are putting in your nose.

All the white parents, even those who participated in school activities, expressed very little knowledge of the school curriculum and policies. Despite their satisfaction, they did mention specifically that they were dissatisfied with, or had reservations about discipline, especially the behaviour of other children. Many of the parents had visited school at some point to discuss conflict between their child and other children. The other reservations parents expressed were related to teaching and curriculum.

Over half the parents whose children attended the nursery school felt that it had not prepared their children adequately for the transition to the middle school. A parent of a child at Castle School explained:

To me they seem to play more than work. You see when we went to school all the writing was drummed into you. Now it seems as though they are doing something for half an hour and then a lot more of it is put into chatting. I mean she comes home with little things that she says. It seems as though there is a lot more playtime than work. It wouldn't help when she moves to the big school.

And a parent of a child at Dewry School said:

They [children] do find problems going into juniors actually because there they all sit behind a desk and they can't get up and walk about. The teachers in the first year had quite a few headaches getting them to sit down and getting them to concentrate. At the first school, if they want to they can go and work in the kitchen or anywhere they like. Now in a way I suppose the discipline isn't there for the juniors. For the middle school they can get a bit of a shock when they go there. It takes a little bit of adjusting to.

A few white parents expressed strong reservations about the school's multicultural approach. For example, this parent with a child at Bridgeway School asserted:

One thing I have seen over there is this Eid thing. Indian Christmas. Well I have never heard anything about Jamaica or Barbados, reflecting that. To introduce it into the British system, I think it is wrong. If they are born into this country, they adapt to this country's way of life. I couldn't go to Pakistan and say I want Church of England over there – they would soon tell me what to do . . . I blame all the do gooders . . . It is mainly these people who don't actually live in an area like this who tend to think oh we should be doing this and that . . . it is mostly down in London where you get it a lot. And yet some of them they live in a right middle class all white area . . . and it's all right for them saying that. They might be miles away from a black town. They probably wouldn't live next to one themselves.

A dilemma faced by all the schools in their endeavour to promote multicultural education was, on one hand, the accusation from black parents of tokenistic nods in the direction of multicultural education (as indicated in the comments of the Asian parents) and, on the other hand, white parents expressing concern that black children were being favoured at the expense of white children.

90

Summary

A sample of parents of black and white children were interviewed in order to find out their views on the school, their contact involvement and experience of the school.

A greater proportion of white parents than black parents said that they were likely to participate in school activities such as Parent Workshops. White parents were generally satisfied with the school. The Asian parents expressed satisfaction with both the teaching and the standard of work at the school. In contrast, a large proportion of the Afro-Caribbean parents expressed dissatisfaction with these areas. Both the Afro-Caribbean and Asian parents saw race relations in the school as an area of concern. Asian parents were particularly distressed by the level of racial hostility experienced by their children. Afro-Caribbean parents, on the other hand, complained about their children experiencing racial prejudice from the teachers.

CHAPTER 5

Educational Performance

Thus far the focus has been on the experience of child in the nursery and primary settings in terms of teacher expectation, peer relations, school–home interactions and the school system. How do these features relate, if at all, to the central aim of the school: developing the educational potential and achievement of the child?

The general pattern to emerge from studies of the educational performance of different ethnic groups is that black children obtain significantly lower scores than white children (Swann, 1985; Smith and Tomlinson, 1989; Drew and Gray, 1990). This difference in scores has usually been explained in terms of black 'underachievement'. However, the use and appropriateness of the term 'underachievement' is itself problematic. Several writers have noted that there is a danger that the concept of 'underachievement' has come to be accepted as a taken for granted fact 'rather than as a problem that requires sensitive and systematic integration' (Troyna, 1984). Therefore, it could be that Afro-Caribbean pupils' underachievement becomes a self-fulfilling prophecy. It could constitute a set of negative views which teachers, administrators and policy makers may use to label pupils and absolve themselves of responsibility.

Another problem in interpreting the wealth of information on the 'performance' of different ethnic groups is that the information is often derived from secondary schools. It is therefore difficult to obtain a sense of progression from the primary school and it is difficult to discern patterns of performance in the school careers of different groups. In an attempt to rectify this deficiency Wright (1986), in her study of the secondary school experiences of ethnic

91

minority pupils, analysed the performance of a whole year group. Using the results of reading test scores on entering the secondary school, she found that Afro-Caribbean pupils had the highest average reading scores of all pupil groups. Yet Afro-Caribbean pupils completed their secondary school careers with fewer school-leaving qualifications than other groups.

By contrast, Smith and Tomlinson (1989) reported in their study of *The School Effect*:

> earlier in the pupils' secondary school careers, attainment tests had indicated that 'West Indian' and South Asian children had entered the schools with lower than average scores in reading and maths (p. 265).

However, they found that at the end of the pupils' secondary school careers the average performance of different ethnic groups was found to replicate the pattern revealed by the studies cited above, i.e. that of white pupils gaining the highest number of qualifications.

The purpose of this chapter is to examine the performance of different ethnic groups on tests given at their first school and middle school respectively. The results are from year groups at Bridgeway First School, Castle First School and Dewry Middle School. Because of the small numbers of black pupils involved the results are not analysed by gender. There is an intention to analyse the results by reference to:

(1) The extent to which poor teacher–pupil relationships experienced by Afro-Caribbean pupils has had an effect.
(2) The extent to which the observations of teachers that Afro-Caribbean pupils were of high ability but 'underachieving' are borne out.
(3) The extent to which teachers' views that Asian pupils were the most highly motivated group is reflected in the scores.

The academic performance of the children is analysed in Figures 5.1 to 5.5. The tests used by the schools included a standardised reading test, undertaken prior to the children's transfer to the middle school, and the performance on the Richmond Tests taken by all children across the whole year group in the middle school.

Reading performance on transfer

At the end of the final year, before the children transferred to the middle school, the first school tested their reading ability. Both schools used the same test.

Figures 5.1(a) and (b) present the results of this test. In Bridgeway First School three-quarters of the Afro-Caribbean children had a Reading Age (RA) on or above their chronological age (CA). By contrast, just under half of white children had a RA equal to or above their CA. The Asian children's results, however, showed a majority with a RA below their CA.

Figure 5.1 Reading age and chronological age

(a) Bridgeway First School, age 8

Ethnic group	Total no. of pupils	On or above CA	0–6 mths below CA	6 mths–2 yrs below CA	Over 2 yrs below CA
Asian	12	2	2	5	3
Afro-Caribbean	13	10	0	2	1
White	19	9	0	10	0
Total	44	21	2	17	4

(b) Castle First School, age 8

Ethnic group	Total no. of pupils	On or above CA	0–6 mths below CA	6 mths–2 yrs below CA	Over 2 yrs below CA
Asian	11	3	1	0	7
Afro-Caribbean	12	6	0	1	5
White	20	6	5	2	7
Total	43	15	6	3	19

In Castle First School, the Afro-Caribbean children were again the only group where one-half of them had a RA on or above their CA. The Asian children were again well below the reading age for their years with over 60 per cent more than two years behind.

In both schools the white and Asian children had the lowest figures for a reading age on or above their chronological age.

Performance on Richmond Tests of basic skills: Dewry Middle School

At the end of the academic year children of all year groups were tested on the Richmond Tests of basic skills. The tests were organised by levels related to chronological age. The majority of children at this school would have been at Bridgeway or Castle schools previously. These tests may therefore give some indication of the academic progress from junior to middle school. The results shown on Figures 5.2 to 5.5 cover the children's performance on English language and maths problem solving.

Figure 5.2 Performance on Richmond Tests of basic skills: Dewry Middle School Level 1 (8–9 years)

(a) Test: Vocabulary (mean score = 90, national mean = 100)

Ethnic group	Total no. of pupils	Over 100	100–90	Below 90
Asian	3	0	2	1
Afro-Caribbean	6	2	2	2
White	23	9	7	7
Total	32	11	11	10

(b) Test: Reading Comprehension (mean score = 89, national mean = 100)

Ethnic group	Total no. of pupils	Over 100	100–89	Below 89
Asian	3	0	1	2
Afro-Caribbean	6	2	0	4
White	23	9	5	9
Total	32	11	6	15

(c) Test: Spelling (mean score = 94, national mean = 100)

Ethnic group	Total no. of pupils	Over 100	100–94	Below 94
Asian	3	0	2	1
Afro-Caribbean	6	3	0	3
White	23	10	1	12
Total	32	13	3	16

(d) Test: Maths problem solving (mean score = 93, national mean = 100)

Ethnic group	Total no. of pupils	Over 100	100–93	Below 93
Asian	3	1	2	0
Afro-Caribbean	6	3	1	2
White	23	13	2	8
Total	32	17	5	10

Figures 5.2(a)–(d) show the performance on these tests for 8–9 year olds. They show no major variations between the ethnic groups.

Figures 5.3(a)–(d) show the performance on these tests for 9–10 year olds. On all the language tests it is clear that the Afro-Caribbean children were performing better than other ethnic groups. They are the only group with over half of them obtaining scores above the mean on all of the language tests. For the white and Asian children over half of them have scores below the mean on all three language tests. On the maths test all three groups have a very similar distribution of scores.

Figures 5.4(a)–(d) show the performance on these tests for the 10–11 year age group. On all the language tests the Asian children have the lowest proportion of scores of over 100 and they are over-

Figure 5.3 Performance on Richmond Tests of basic skills: Dewry Middle School Level 2 (9–10 years)

(a) Test: Vocabulary (mean score = 95, national mean = 100)

Ethnic group	Total no. of pupils	Over 100	100–95	Below 95
Asian	7	1	2	4
Afro-Caribbean	9	5	2	2
White	25	5	5	15
Total	41	11	9	21

(b) Test: Reading Comprehension (mean score = 99, national mean = 100)

Ethnic group	Total no. of pupils	99 and over	Below 99
Asian	7	3	4
Afro-Caribbean	9	6	3
White	25	10	15
Total	41	19	22

(c) Test: Spelling (mean score = 99, national mean = 100)

Ethnic group	Total no. of pupils	99 and over	Below 99
Asian	7	4	3
Afro-Caribbean	9	6	3
White	25	11	14
Total	41	21	20

(d) Test: Maths problem solving (mean score = 101, national mean = 100)

Ethnic group	Total no. of pupils	101 and over	Below 101
Asian	7	3	4
Afro-Caribbean	9	5	4
White	25	12	13
Total	41	20	21

represented in scores below the mean. It is again the Afro-Caribbean children who have the highest proportion of scores above the mean on all of the language tests. On the maths test the Asian children are the only group with half of pupils gaining scores above the mean. The results for the Afro-Caribbean and white pupils are very similar on this test.

Figures 5.5(a)–(d) show the performance on these tests for the 11–12 year age group. The tables reveal that on all of the language tests the great majority of the Asian children have scores below the mean. For the Afro-Caribbean and white children the distribution of scores is proportionately similar on the vocabulary and reading comprehension tests. However, the performance of the white pupils is proportionately much better on the spelling test than the Afro-

Figure 5.4 Performance on Richmond Tests of basic skills: Dewry Middle School Level 3 (10–11 years)

(a) Test: Vocabulary (mean score = 89, national mean = 100)

Ethnic group	Total no. of pupils	Over 100	100–89	Below 89
Asian	4	0	3	1
Afro-Caribbean	9	1	6	2
White	16	3	6	7
Total	29	4	15	10

(b) Test: Reading Comprehension (mean score = 93, national mean = 100)

Ethnic group	Total no. of pupils	Over 100	100–93	Below 93
Asian	4	0	0	4
Afro-Caribbean	9	2	3	4
White	16	3	5	8
Total	29	5	8	16

(c) Test: Spelling (mean score = 95, national mean = 100)

Ethnic group	Total no. of pupils	Over 100	100–95	Below 95
Asian	4	1	0	3
Afro-Caribbean	9	4	1	4
White	16	4	4	8
Total	29	9	5	15

(d) Test: Maths problem solving (mean score = 100, national mean = 100)

Ethnic group	Total no. of pupils	Above 100	Below 100
Asian	4	2	2
Afro-Caribbean	9	4	5
White	16	6	10
Total	29	12	17

Caribbean children. However, there are only five of the latter. On the maths test the white children are the only group with over half of the pupils obtaining scores above the mean.

When considering the overall performance of the three groups over the four-year groups one has to be cautious in interpreting the information because of the relatively small numbers of Asians and Afro-Caribbean. However, overall of all of the groups the Afro-Caribbean children show a slightly better performance on the reading and language tests. This replicates the scores of this group on Reading Age in the last year of junior school. Statistically, the Afro-Caribbeans continue to have the higher proportionate scores in English language tests both in the last years of junior school and up to year 11–12 of the middle school. If there is a statistical change

Figure 5.5 Performance on Richmond Tests of basic skills: Dewry Middle School Level 4 (11–12 years)

(a) Test: Vocabulary (mean score = 95, national mean = 100)

Ethnic group	Total no. of pupils	Over 100	100–95	Below 95
Asian	12	0	2	10
Afro-Caribbean	5	1	2	2
White	24	9	8	7
Total	41	10	12	19

(b) Test: Reading Comprehension (mean score = 96, national mean = 100)

Ethnic group	Total no. of pupils	Over 100	100–95	Below 95
Asian	12	1	2	9
Afro-Caribbean	5	1	1	3
White	24	8	4	12
Total	41	10	7	24

(c) Test: Spelling (mean score = 94, national mean = 100)

Ethnic group	Total no. of pupils	Over 100	100–95	Below 95
Asian	12	0	3	9
Afro-Caribbean	5	1	0	4
White	24	8	4	12
Total	41	9	7	25

(d) Test: Maths problem solving (mean score = 97, national mean = 100)

Ethnic group	Total no. of pupils	Over 100	100–95	Below 95
Asian	12	2	1	9
Afro-Caribbean	5	1	0	4
White	24	11	3	10
Total	41	14	4	23

through the year groups for Afro-Caribbeans it appears to be year 11–12 when their performance in spelling and reading is proportionately lower than for white and Asian pupils. (Although this does not apply to vocabulary test scores.)

The Asian children consistently scored the lowest on reading and language tests. In the last year of junior school this group had the lowest proportions on or above the reading age. The proportion of Asian pupils obtaining scores on or above the mean for vocabulary, reading and spelling does not improve statistically through the four-year groups of the middle school. If anything, their performance in years 11–12 is often worse than earlier year groups – particularly for vocabulary and spelling.

The performance scores of the white children do not seem to

change much during the years. Although it should be noted that the proportion of pupils with scores on or above the mean on the language tests in the middle school is greater than the proportion on or above the reading age in the last year of the junior schools. This is the only group where this appears to be the case. Through the years of the middle school the only significant statistical change in the performance scores of this group appears to be in vocabulary, where in year 11-12 the proportion of pupils on or above the mean is lower than for the group age groups. This change is also common to the other two ethnic groups.

As regards the performance on the maths test, the proportion of Afro-Caribbean pupils obtaining scores on or above the mean was similar to or above that of the other two groups from years 8-9 to 10-11. However, this proportion falls below the other two groups for age group 11-12. This proportionate performance overall in maths is slightly below that of the English language tests. For the Asian pupils this situation is reversed as it appears to be for the white pupils. It is noticeable that both of these groups generally have a lower performance score distribution in maths in year 11-12 than most younger year groups.

It must be stressed that the analysis presented above is statistical by year group and not an analysis of the same pupils through the year groups, thus the comments concerning change of performance with age must be tentative.

Summary

The conclusions of this chapter must be:

(1) There is no evidence that the poor teacher–pupil relationships experienced by Afro-Caribbean pupils have had an effect on their test score performance. The only possible exception could be in year 11-12. This is not to say that the scores would not have been higher without this poor relationship, but the effect does not seem to have resulted in any relatively poorer performance of this group compared with Asian and white pupils.

(2) There is no evidence that the observations by teachers that Afro-Caribbean pupils were of high ability but 'underachieving' is borne out. In terms of their performance relative to that of other groups there is no evidence of 'underachievement'.

(3) There is no evidence that the views of teachers that Asians are the most highly motivated group is reflected in test score performance. In none of the tests do the Asian pupils consistently perform better than the other two groups. In terms of the Asian children, however, it could be tentatively concluded that their school is a factor in their educational performance.

CHAPTER 6

Conclusions

The nursery, first schools and the middle school studied are similar to many schools of their kind in inner-city areas. The schools are committed to equality of education and many of the staff are 'caring'. In addition, the local education authority has carefully devised policies designed to promote equality of opportunity for all children and 'good race relations'. The policies have been followed through with support and training for staff.

An examination of the experience of black children at the schools in terms of teacher perceptions and treatment of children, peer relations, relations with auxiliary staff, 'strategies of discipline and control, and parent teacher relations, highlighted issues which clearly raise questions about the efficacy of both schools' and the LEA's policies in the area of 'race relations'.

Within the classroom, from the nursery to the upper primary classroom, in terms of teachers' attitudes and classroom practices, observations revealed that there are processes at work – sometimes unintentional and at other times motivated by the best intentions – which nevertheless have the result of discriminating against black children in the nursery/primary classroom. Both Afro-Caribbean and Asian children faced negative teacher interaction in the classroom. But the teachers operated different negative assumption for different groups of children. For the Asian children, particularly the younger children, the assumptions were about their English language skills, poor social skills and their inability to socialise with other groups of children in the classroom. However, teachers' expressed views revealed assumptions of Asian children and their parents which were

100

also positive. Teachers expect children of Asian origins to be industrious, courteous and keen to learn. They also tend to assume that Asian children are well-disciplined, highly motivated children from family backgrounds where educational success is highly valued.

Afro-Caribbean children, by contrast, (especially boys) were considered by teachers to exhibit disruptive behaviour in class. Consequently, Afro-Caribbean children were frequently among the most reprimanded and controlled group in the classroom. Further, it was observed that Afro-Caribbean were likely to be singled out for reprimanding even where several children of different groups were engaged in the same act or behaviour. It was not surprising therefore, to find that Afro-Caribbean children were over-represented in the schools' disciplinary system. Just as they did in relation to Asian children, teachers, therefore, held stereotypes of Afro-Caribbean children which tended to be totally negative; more significantly, teachers' negative expectations transcended their judgements of these children's ability.

Overall, the negative assumptions held by teachers for different groups (that is, assumptions about Asian children's English language skills and about Afro-Caribbean children's disruptive behaviour) derived from the perceived threat that both groups – the Asian children to a lesser extent – were supposed to pose for classroom management and teacher effectiveness.

It was also revealed that school curricula do not always accommodate religious and cultural demands. For instance, it was observed that Muslim girls were often placed in a situation where the values of their families conflicted with the requirements of the school. Also teachers' efforts to promote multiculturalism in the classroom via the curriculum content were often doubted by the black children. Further it was observed that this approach often provoked intolerance among different groups of children.

The evidence provided on the relationship between the children themselves within the classroom shows that victimisation was a common experience for many Asian children. Racist name-calling by white peers was part of their daily classroom life. The treatment which Asian children received from white peers proved to be a further source of classroom insecurity for this group. Racial harassment, which involved both verbal and physical attacks by white peers, was also the daily experience of Asian children outside the classroom, for example, in the playground. Staff were aware of the racial harassment experienced by Asian children, but were reluctant to formally address this situation. On the other hand the Afro-Caribbean children's 'around the school experience' was characterised by further conflict with staff, in particular with the auxiliary staff.

Data from observations and interviews showed marked differences between black and white parents in their dealings and views of the school. Asian parents expressed satisfaction with quality of teaching in the school; however, they expressed dissatisfaction with what they considered to be the school's tokenistic approach to cultural diversity and the ineffectual school responses to racial harassment. The Afro-Caribbean parents were dissatisfied with the school and were among the parents who regularly visited the school (often by invitation) in order to express their feelings in this regard. Afro-Caribbean parents often complained of injustice which they felt their children experienced at the hands of teachers. Staff responded by assuming that the claim was at best an error and at worst a smokescreen meant to draw attention away from a genuine offence. Finally, white parents were generally satisfied with the school; however, some parents expressed reservations about the teaching methods. Some parents felt that even the very young children in the classroom, at lesson time, should be seated at a desk and there was disapproval of multicultural education: the feeling was that the curriculum content favoured black children.

The scores of different groups of children, for example, children in their final year at Bridgeway and Castle and all year groups at Dewry School, on various standardised tests (i.e. reading tests, numeracy tests and so on) were analysed. On the reading tests, for instance, Afro-Caribbean children performed overall slightly better than other groups; whereas Asian children's performance was marginally lower than other groups.

Overall, the findings highlight the complexity of classroom and school life in the multiracial and predominantly white context. Moreover, they confirm the view of Parekh (1985) and others concerning the fallacies which often underpin debates regarding the existence of racism in schools. Black children of Afro-Caribbean and Asian origins experience school in similar but also in very different ways, some of which are highlighted above. In both cases, the children's ethnicity influenced their interaction with staff and their experience of staff expectations. Only in the case of the Asian children did ethnicity appear to be a direct influence on their relations with their classmate.

The basic lesson to emerge from the data above, therefore, is that there is evidence of poor 'race relations' in inner-city primary schools, and ultimately it shows that 'race relations' is an issue for schools. Those who still advocate colour-blind approaches in schools are avoiding the reality that staff, like most other people, do treat people differently on the basis of perceived 'racial' characteristics. Further, many nursery and primary staff are still reluctant to accept that younger children can hold incipient racist attitudes and exhibit hostility towards members of other groups. In the remainder of the chapter attention is turned to suggestions for promoting 'good race-relations' in education, particularly in early education. In particular, it is concerned with what can be done at institutional and classroom level: in the former, emphasis is placed on specific school policy and in the latter on classroom management issues. However, this is not to deny the obvious mutual dependency between the school and the classroom in 'race-relations' matters. Indeed, it recognises that at each of these levels, there are similar processes in operation. Yet it is also clear that the school and the classroom level give rise to specific issues.

At the school level

The evidence presented in this book shows that racism is a crucial issue for both multiracial and predominantly white primary schools. The Swann Report (1985) asserted that education had:

> ...a major role to play in countering racism which still persists in Britain today...A crucial element is to seek to identify and remove practices and procedures which work, directly or indirectly, and intentionally or unintentionally, against pupils from any ethnic group, and to promote, through the curriculum, an appreciation and commitment to the principles of equality and justice, on the part of all pupils.

More recently, The Children Act stated:

> ...children from a very young age learn about different races and cultures including religion and languages and will be capable of assigning different values to them. It is important that people working with young children are aware of this, so that their practice enables the children to develop positive attitudes to differences of race, culture and language. (HMSO, 1991)

Such statements point to the need for a strong and clear school policy in order to ensure equality of opportunity for all children. It is evident from the study of the four schools that the issue of racial harassment is an area which needs to be addressed by a whole school policy.

Racial harassment (which includes physical abuse and racist calling) can be reduced in schools if the schools take a strong and clear position against it, but the policy must be well known by all children. The headteacher's role is extremely important in facilitating this, so that children can see the commitment shown. However, there can be problems, particularly if children perceive that teachers do not have the same commitment. This is exhibited when black children find that teachers do not listen to them when they complain of racist incidents.

Furthermore, a school policy may be effective within the school but not outside, where the development of racist ideology continues and thrives. This suggests that policies designed to combat racist incidents inside the school need to exist side by side with the treatment of 'race' in the curriculum. It is the underlying roots of racism that need challenging. Multicultural education has been the major strategy employed by schools to achieve this. However, it can have unintended consequences. For example, it can create hostility amongst white children who may perceive ethnic minority cultures as having more value than their own and it can lead to embarrassment amongst black children. It may also not be unproblematic to continually define the issues involved in terms of 'race'. Rather than organising children's experiences around 'racial' definitions of the real world, the curriculum and teachers need to address the real experiences that children bring with them into the classroom. It is not impossible for children to comprehend the issues involved in the production of racism by referring to its origins in social structure and by using notions of equality that many children possess.

It is suggested therefore than an effective school policy must not simply be that of the headteacher's but of all staff. The policy must be seen to be firm and involve all groups of children who experience hostility. The curriculum must be informed by issues of inequality and injustice whose roots lie in the social processes outside the school so that children gain an understanding of the wider issues and effects of racist behaviour.

The employment of a greater proportion of black groups within the teaching profession (and also at all levels of the profession) would provide positive role models for both staff and children, while simultaneously helping to facilitate a better understanding between schools and the communities which they serve. But the presence of black teachers in itself is not enough to bring about the necessary improved school ethos and practices. Further, it is important to note that black teachers are no more experts on multicultural and anti-racist issues than any others and therefore should not be type-cast in this role.

Further, having a policy document is one thing, putting it into practice is quite another. The effectiveness of the policy should be regularly monitored and reviewed. This could be achieved through both a series of questions to be discussed and tasks to be undertaken by the staff. This form of staff development is crucial in any attempts at improving the overall quality of the school's work.

Classroom management issues

The classroom has a crucial role in the promotion of 'good race relations'. It is the responsibility of teachers to create a positive and supportive classroom climate where all children can flourish. Observations of how black children experience schooling from the nursery through to the upper junior showed that some teachers are likely to have developed stereotypes of black children. For instance, within the classroom Afro-Caribbean children became identified as 'aggressive' and 'disruptive': in other words a classroom management problem. Such views came to inform teachers' practice and general interaction with Afro-Caribbean children. Thus, teachers in their dealings with these children used selective management strategies, which ranged from frequent verbal reprimands to physical chastisement. Such perspectives and consequent actions, however, were not confined to teachers who could be loosely described as 'authoritarian' but were also evident among more 'liberal' teachers (Mac an Ghaill, 1988).

Another feature of classroom life which revealed teacher insecurity and frustration was working with bilingual and multilingual children. Bilingual children were considered to be a problem in the classroom rather than an advantage.

In a sense the management styles adopted by teachers working in ethnically and linguistically mixed classrooms, which include the adoption of racial stereotypes, authoritarian strategies of control and also a tendency to treat bilingualism as an obstacle to learning, partly reflect a situation where teachers feel that they are forced to 'manage' children for whom they are inadequately prepared. Criticisms have been made about the failure of both initial and in-service teacher education to meet the professional needs of teachers in a multiracial and multi-ethnic society (Rampton Report, 1991; Keele Report, 1981; Swann, 1985). For example, the Keele Report on in-service provision for individual teachers speaks of:

> ... the experiences of many of the teachers we have interviewed faced with the day to day and minute by minute problems of working in classroom with children whose cultural, community, intellectual and linguistic situations are diverse and which they only incompletely understand. (pp. 57–8)

Added to the insecurity experienced by white teachers working with children from different ethnic backgrounds are the constraints and demands on teachers resulting from such factors as the imposition of the National Curriculum, together with the general under-resourced nature of inner-city schools.

It is important to stress that if we are not to fall into the trap of simply 'blaming the teacher', we need to recognise and appreciate the insecurity that some white teachers feel about working in ethnically and linguistically mixed classes. In this respect, practitioners require greater support from the education service. Our children need confident and secure teachers. Teacher education has an integral role to play here. In the words of John Eggleston (1983), 'Teachers need practical examples of successful multicultural teaching and not consciousness raising'. As he informs us,

> ... some of the more enlightened teacher training institutions are now coming to see very clearly that it is only when teachers have had the opportunity to experience success with black children are they likely to be ready to respond fully to their courses that are designed to remove such impediments to multicultural teaching as the use of racist books, the assumptions of racial inferiority and the deficiencies of "cultural understanding".

Finally, as Pumfrey *et al.* (1990) remind us:

> If we are to improve race relations in education, all those involved, professionals, parents and pupils, have much to do and much to learn.

References

Aboud, F. (1988) *Children and Prejudice*. Oxford: Basil Blackwell.

Akhtar, S. and Stronach, I. (1986) 'They call me Blacky'. *Times Educational Supplement*, 19 September, 23.

Arora, R. K. and Duncan, C. G. (1986) *Multicultural Education Towards Good Practice*. London: Routledge.

Banton, M. and Harwood, J. (1975) *The Race Concept*. Newton Abbot: David and Charles.

Banton, M. (1977) *The Idea of Race*. London: Tavistock.

Banton (1988) *Racial Consciousness*. London: Longman.

Becker, H. S. (1952) 'Social class variations in the teacher–pupil relationship'. *Journal of Educational Sociology*, Vol. 25, pp. 451–65.

Becker, H. S. (1963) *Outsiders' Studies in the Sociology of Deviance*. New York: Free Press.

Bernstein, B. (1973) *Class, Codes and Control*, Vol. 1. London: Routledge and Kegan Paul.

Brown, C. (1984) *Black and White in Britain*, The Third PSI Survey. London: Heinemann.

Bosser, S. (1979) *Tasks and Social Relationships in the Classroom*. Cambridge University Press.

Brandt, G. (1986) *The Racialisation of Anti-Racist Teaching*. Lewes: Falmer Press.

Burgess, R. G. (1984) *In the Field: An Introduction to Field Research*. London: George Allen and Unwin.

Burrell, G. and Morgan, G. (1979) *Sociological and Organizational Analysis*. London: Heinemann Educational Books.

Carrington, B. and Short, G. (1989) *'Race' and the primary school*. Windsor: NFER–Nelson.

Children Act, The (1991). London: HMSO.

Clarricoates, K. (1981) 'The experience of patriarchal schooling'. *Interchange*, 12, 2/3, pp. 185–206.

107

Clarricoates, K. (1987) 'Child Culture at School, a Clash Between Gendered Worlds' in Pollard, A. (ed.) *Children and their Primary Schools*. Lewes: Falmer Press.

Coard, B. (1977) 'What the British school system does to the black child' in Raynor, J. and Harris, E. (eds) (1977) *Schooling in the city*. London: Ward Lock.

Cohen, L. and Marion, L. (1983) *Multicultural Classrooms*. London: Croom Helm.

Cohen, L. (1989) 'Ignorance, not hostility: student teachers' perceptions of ethnic minorities in Britain' in Verma, G. K. (ed.) *Education For All: A Landmark in Pluralism*. Lewes: Falmer Press.

Commission for Racial Equality (1987) *Racial Attacks: A Survey in Eight Areas of Britain*. London: CRE.

Commission for Racial Equality (1988) *Learning in Terror: A Survey of Racial Harassment in Schools and Colleges*, London: CRE.

Commission for Racial Equality (1989) *Code of Practice for the Elimination of Racial Discrimination in Education*. London: CRE.

Corrigan, P. (1989) *Schooling the Smash Street Kids*. London: Macmillan.

Davey, A. (1983) *Learning to be Prejudiced*. London: Edward Arnold.

Denscombe, M. (1980) 'Keeping 'em quiet' in Woods, P. (ed.) *Teacher Strategies*. London: Croom Helm.

Department of Education and Science (1985) *Education for All*. London: HMSO.

Department of Education and Science (1982) *The New Teacher and School: A Report*. London: HMSO.

Douglas, J. B. (1964) *Home and School*. London: MacGibbon and Kee.

Edwards, V. and Redfern, A. (1988) *At Home in School, Parent Participation in Primary Education*. London and New York: Routledge.

Drew, D. and Gray, J. (1990) 'The black–white gap in exam achievement: a statistical critique of a decade's research'. Paper presented at the British Sociological Association annual conference, Social Division and Social Change, University of Surrey.

Eggleston, S. J. *et al.* (1981) *In-Service Teacher Education in a Multiracial Society*. Keele: University of Keele.

Eggleston, J. 'Ethnic naivety'. *Times Educational Supplement*, 11 March 1983.

Elton, Lord (1989) *Discipline in School: Report of the Committee of Enquiry*. London: HMSO.

Figueroa, P. M. E. (1984) 'Race relations and cultural differences: Some ideas on a racist frame of reference' in Verma, G. K. and Bagley, C. (eds) *Race Relations and Cultural Differences*. London: Croom.

Flanders, N. A. (1970) *Analysing Teaching Behaviour*. New York: Addison Wesley.

Gaine, C. (1987) *No Problem Here: A Practical Approach to Education and Race in White Schools*. London: Hutchinson.

Galton, M., Simon, B. and Croll, P. (1980) *Inside the Primary Classroom*. London: Routledge and Kegan Paul.

Gillborn, D. (1990) *'Race', Ethnicity and Education*. London: Unwin Hyman.

Gilroy, P. (1987) *There ain't no Black in the Union Jack*. London: Hutchinson.

Glaser, B. G. and Strauss, A. L. (1967) *The Discovery of Grounded Theory*. London: Weidenfeld & Nicolson.

Green, P. A. (1983b) 'Male and female created He them'. *Multicultural Teaching*, Vol. 2, no. 1, Autumn, pp. 4–7.

Green, P. (1985) 'Multi-ethnic teaching and the pupils' self-concept'. Annex to chapter 2 of *Education for All*, the Final Report of the Committee of Inquiry into the Education of Children from Ethnic Minority Groups. London: HMSO.

Hammersley, M. and Woods, P. (eds) (1976) *The Process of Schooling*. London: Routledge and Kegan Paul.

Hammersley, M. and Atkinson, P. (1983) *Ethnography: Principles in Practice*. London: Routledge.

Hargreaves, A. (1985) 'The Micro-macro Problem in the Sociology of Education' in Burgess, R. G. (ed) *Issues in Educational Research*. Lewes: Falmer Press.

Hargreaves, D. H. (1967) *Social Relations in a Secondary School*. London: Routledge and Kegan Paul.

Hargreaves, D. H. (1972) *Interpersonal Relations and Education*. London: Routledge and Kegan Paul.

Hargreaves, D. H., Hestor, S. K. and Mellor, F. J. (1975) *Deviance in Classrooms*. London: Routledge and Kegan Paul.

Her Majesty's Inspectorate (1984) *Race Relations in Schools: A Summary of Discussions at Meetings in Five Local Authorities*. London: DES.

Home Affairs Committee (1989) *Racial Attacks and Harassment: First Report*. London: HMSO.

Husband, C. (1987) (ed.) *'Race' in Britain: Continuity and Change* 2nd edition. London: Hutchinson.

Jackson, P. (1968) *Life in Classrooms*. New York: Holt, Rinehart and Winston.

Kelly, E. and Cohn, T. (1988) *Racism in Schools – New Research Evidence*. Stoke: Trentham Books.

Kelly, E. (1990) 'Use and Abuse of Racial Language in Secondary Schools' in Pumfrey, P. D. and Verma, G. K. (eds) *Race Relations and Urban Education*. Lewes: Falmer Press.

Kutnick, P. (1988) *Relationships in the Primary School Classroom*. London: Paul Chapman Publishing.

Leicester, M. (1986) 'Multicultural curriculum or antiracist education: denying the guilt'. *Multicultural Teaching*, 4, 2.

Leiter, K. (1974) 'Ad hocing in the Schools' in Ciconvel, A. V. (ed.) *Language Use and School Performance*. New York: Academic Press.

Lynch, J. (1984) 'Curriculum and Assessment in Craft' in *Education and Cultural Pluralism*. Lewes: Falmer Press.

Macdonald, I., Bhavnani, R., Khan, L. and John, G. (1989) *Murder in the Playground: The Report of the Macdonald Inquiry into Racism and Racial Violence in Manchester Schools*. London: Longsight Press.

Mac an Ghail, M. (1988) *Young, Gifted and Black: student-teacher relations in the schooling of black youth*. Milton Keynes: Open University Press.

Matza, D. (1964) *Delinquency and Drift*. New York: Wiley.

Matza, D. (1969) *Becoming Deviant*. Englewood Cliffs: Prentice Hall.

Miles, R. (1982) *Racism and Migrant Labour*. London: Routledge and Kegan Paul.

Miles, R. and Solomos, J. (1987) 'Migration and the state in Britain: a historical overview' in Husband, C. (ed.) *'Race' in Britain: Continuity and Change* 2nd edition. London: Hutchinson.

Miles, R. (1988) 'Racialization' in Cashmore, E. (ed.) *Dictionary of Race and Ethnic Relations*. 2nd edition. London: Routledge.

Miles, R. (1989) *Racism*. London: Routledge.

Milner, D. (1983) *Children and Race: Ten Years On*. London: Ward Lock.

Moreno, J. L. (1953) *Who Shall Survive? Foundations of Sociometry Group*. New York: Beacon House.

Mortimore, P., Sammons, P., Stoll, L., Lewis, D. and Ecols R. (1988) *School Matters: the junior years*. Wells, Somerset: Open Books.

Mullard, C. (1984) *Anti-Racist Education: The Three O's*, London: National Association for Multi-Racial Education.

Opie, I. and Opie, P. (1969) *Children's Games in Street and Playground*. London and New York: Oxford University Press.

Parekh, B. (1985) 'Background to the West Indian tragedy'. *Times Educational Supplement*, 22 March.

Parekh, B. (1986) 'The concept of multicultural education' in Modgil, S., Verma, G. K., Mallick, K. and Modgil, C. *Multicultural Education: The Interminable Debate*. London: Falmer Press.

Plowden, B. (1967) *Children and their primary schools*. London: HMSO.

Pollard, A. (1980) 'Teacher interest and changing situations of survival threat in primary school classrooms', in Woods, P. (ed.) *Teacher Strategies*. London: Croom Helm.

Pollard, A. (1985) *The Social World of the Primary School*. London: Holt, Rinehart and Winston.

Pumfrey, P. D. and Verma, G. K. (eds) *Race Relations and Urban Education*. Lewes: Falmer Press.

Rampton Report: Department of Education and Science (1981) *West Indian Children in our Schools*. London: HMSO.

Rex, J. and Mason, D. (1986) (eds) *Theories of Race and Ethnic Relations*. Cambridge University Press.

Richardson, R. (1989) 'Materials, resources and methods' in Cole, M. (ed.) *Education for Equality: Some guidelines for good practice*. London: Routledge.

Riseborough, G. F. (1981) 'Teacher careers and comprehensive schooling: an empirical study'. *Sociology*, Vol. 15, no. 3. pp. 352-81.

Riseborough, G. F. (1985) 'Pupils, teachers' careers and schooling: an empirical study', in Ball, S. J. and Goodson, I. F. (eds.) *Teachers' Lives and Career*. Lewes: Falmer Press.

Rist, R. C. (1970) 'Student social class and teacher expectations: the self-fulfilling prophecy in ghetto education'. *Harvard Education Review*, 40, pp. 411-51.

Rosenthal, R. and Jacobson, L. (1968) *Pygmalion in the Classroom: Teacher Expectations and Pupils' Intellectual Development*. New York: Holt, Rinehart and Winston.

Rutler, M., Maughan, B., Mortimore, P. and Ouston, J. (1979) *Fifteen Thousand Hours*. London: Open Books.

Schutz, A. (1944) 'The Stranger'. *American Journal of Sociology*. Vol. 49, No. 6.

Schutz, A. (1970) *On Phenomenology of the Social World*. London: Heinemann.

Sharp, R. and Green, A. (1975) *Education and Social Control: study in progressive primary education*. London: Routledge and Kegan Paul.

Sivanandon, A. (1985) 'RAT and the degradation of the black struggle'. *Race and Class*, **26**, pp. 1-3.

Slavin, R. (1983) *Cooperative Learning*. Longman: New York.

Sluckin, A. (1981) *Growing up in the Playground*. London: Routledge and Kegan Paul.

Smith, D. J. and Tomlinson, S. (1989) *The School Effect*. London: Policy Studies.

Spencer, D. (1987) 'Racist names hurt more than sticks and stones'. *Times Educational Supplement*, 18 September.

Spencer, D. (1988) 'Panel finds teachers guilty of bigotry'. *Times Educational Supplement*, 20 May.

Stanworth, M. (1983) *Gender and Schooling: A Study of Sexual Divisions in the Classroom*. London: Hutchinson.

Stebbins, R. A. (1981) 'Classroom ethnography and the definition of the situation' in Barton, L. and Walker, S. (eds) *School, Teachers and Teaching*. Lewes: Falmer Press.

Stone, M. (1980) *The Education of the Black Child in Britain*. London: Fontana.

Swann, M. (1985) *Education for All*. Final Report of the Committee of Inquiry into the Education of Children from Ethnic Minority Groups (Cmnd 9453). London: HMSO.

Tizard, B., Blatchford, P., Burke, J., Farquhar, C. and Plewis, I. Young (1988) *Children at School in the Innercity*. London: Lawrence Erlbaum.

Tomlinson, S. (1981) *Educational Subnormality: A Study in Decision-Making*. London: Routledge and Kegan Paul.

Tomlinson, S. (1983) *Ethnic Minorities in British Schools*. London: Heinemann.

Tomlinson, S. (1984) *Special Education and Social Interests*. London: Croom Helm.

Troyna, B. (1984) 'Fact or artefact? The "educational underachievement" of black pupils'. *British Journal of Sociology of Education*, Vol. 5, no. 2, pp. 153–66.

Troyna, B. and Williams, J. (1986) *Racism, Education and the State: the Racialization of Education Policy*. Beckenham: Croom Helm.

Willis, P. (1977) *Learning to Labour*. Farnborough: Saxon House.

Woods, P. (1977) 'Teaching For Survival' in Woods P. and Hammersley, M. (eds) *School Experience*. London: Croom Helm.

Woods, P. (1979) *The Divided School*. London: Routledge and Kegan Paul.

Woods, P. (1985) 'Ethnography and theory construction in educational research' in Burgess, R. (ed.) *Field Methods in the Study of Education*. Lewes: Falmer Press.

Woods, P. (1986) *Inside Schools: ethnography in educational research*. London: Routledge and Kegan Paul.

Wright, C. (1986) 'School Processes: An Ethnographic Study' in Eggleson, J., Dunn, J. and Madju, A. *Education for Some*. London: Trentham Books.

Wright, C. (1987) 'Black students – White teachers' in Troyna, B. (ed.) *Racial Inequality in Education*. London: Tavistock.

Wright, C. (1992) 'Early Education: Multiracial Classrooms' in Gill, D., Maynor, B. and Blair, M. *Racism and Education: Structures and Strategies*. London: Sage.

Index